Unit 2

Interactive
Practice Book *e*

Hampton-Brown

EDGE

Reading, Writing & Language

NATIONAL
GEOGRAPHIC
LEARNING | CENGAGE
Learning

Acknowledgments

Grateful acknowledgment is given to the authors, artists, photographers, museums, publishers, and agents for permission to reprint copyrighted material. Every effort has been made to secure the appropriate permission. If any omissions have been made or if corrections are required, please contact the Publisher.

Photographic Credits

Cover: The "Unisphere" Sculpture Celebrates Humanity's Interdependence, Queens, New York, USA, James P. Blair. Photograph © James P. Blair/National Geographic Stock. **X (1)** Frank Romero. **1** (tr) ©Steve Prezant/Corbis; (mtr) Image Source/JupiterImages; (mbr) © James Hardy/ PhotoAlto Agency/Getty Images. **6** © Image Source/ Jupiterimages; © dk & dennie cody/Masterfile. **7** © dk & dennie cody/Masterfile. **9** © United Archives GmbH/ Alamy. **11** ©ArenaPal/Topham/The Image Works. **12** © Classic Imag /Alamy. **15** ©Andrew Rich/Getty Images. **17** ©Shulevskyy Volodymyr/Shutterstock. **18** ©Morgan Gaynin Inc. **19** ©Morgan Gaynin Inc. **21** ©Sara Tyson. **22** (bg) ©Sara Tyson; (fg) ©Corbis. **28** ©NA/Alamy; ©iconsight/ Alamy; ©The Mazer Corporation. **30** ©Alexandra Boulat. **31** ©Steve McCurry. **32** ©Steve McCurry; ©Steve McCurry. **33** ©Alexandra Boulat. **34** ©Steve McCurry. **40** ©Yellow Dog Productions/Getty Images. **44** ©Frank Morrison/ Shannon Associates L.L.C; ©Frank Morrison/Shannon Associates L.L.C. **45** ©Frank Morrison/Shannon Associates L.L.C; ©Frank Morrison/Shannon Associates L.L.C; ©Frank Morrison/Shannon Associates L.L.C; ©Frank Morrison/ Shannon Associates L.L.C; ©Frank Morrison/Shannon Associates L.L.C; ©Frank Morrison/Shannon Associates L.L.C. **54** ©Jean-Manuel Duvivier/Munro Campagna. **55** ©Jean-Manuel Duvivier/Munro Campagna. **58** ©Megan Wyeth/Aurora/Getty Images. **66** ©Karen Blessen/Morgan Gaynin Inc. **67** ©Karen Blessen/Morgan Gaynin Inc. **68** ©Marc Muench/CORBIS. **70** ©Marc Muench/CORBIS. **71** (r) ©David Muench/CORBIS; (l) ©David Muench/CORBIS. **78** ©Stock4B/Getty Images. **83** ©Image Source Black/Getty Images. **94** ©Reza Abedini Studio/Reza Abedini. **95** ©Reza Abedini Studio/Reza Abedini. **93** ©Mapping Specialists; Mapping Specialists. **99** ©Anna Kari/In Pictures/Corbis; (tc) ©Mapping Specialists; (tl) ©Mapping Specialists. **100** ©Mapping Specialists; Frederick Breedon/Stringer/Getty Images. **105** ©Spencer Grant/PhotoEdit. **106** ©Chris Vallo/ The Mazer Corporation. **107** ©Chris Vallo/The Mazer Corporation. **109** ©CJ Zea/The Mazer Corporation. **110** ©CJ Zea/The Mazer Corporation. **111** ©CJ Zea/The Mazer Corporation. **118** ©Lew Robertson/Corbis. **122** ©S.D. Nelson; ©S.D. Nelson. **123** ©S.D. Nelson; ©S.D. Nelson; ©S.D. Nelson; ©S.D. Nelson; ©S.D. Nelson. **124** ©Mapping Specialists. **125** ©Carsten Peter/Getty Images. **126** ©Carsten Peter/Getty Images. **127** ©Mapping Specialists. **128** ©Carsten Peter/Getty Images. **129** ©Springfield News-Leader. **140** ©Chris Vallo/The Mazer Corporation. **141** ©mountainpix/Shutterstock. **142** ©Chris Vallo/The Mazer Corporation. **147** ©Jupiter Images/Food Pix/Getty Images. **152** ©Mapping Specialists. **153** ©Dorling Kindersley/DK Images. **163** ©Erin Patrice O'Brien/Taxi/Getty Images. **167** ©Keith Baker/Hampton Brown. **168** ©Keith Baker/Hampton Brown. **169** ©Keith Baker/Hampton Brown.

Acknowledgments continue on page 242.

For product information and technology asistance, contact us at **Cengage Learning Customer & Sales Support, 1-800-354-9706**

For permission to use material from this text or product, submit all requests online at **www.cengage.com/permissions** Further permissions questions can be emailed to **permissionrequest@cengage.com**

National Geographic Learning | Cengage Learning
1 Lower Ragsdale Drive
Building 1, Suite 200
Monterey, CA 93940

Cengage Learning is a leading provider of customized learning solutions with office locations around the globe, including Singapore, the United Kingdom, Australia, Mexico, Brazil, and Japan. Locate your local office at **www.cengage.com/global**.

Visit National Geographic Learning online at **ngl.cengage.com**
Visit our corporate website at **www.cengage.com**

Printer: Quad/Graphics, Versailles, KY

ISBN: 978-12857-60476 (Practice Book)
ISBN: 978-12857-60483 (Practice Book Teacher's Annotated Edition)

Printed in the United States of America
18 19 20 21 22
10 9 8 7 6

Unit 4

Unit 6

Unit Vocabulary

Circle a number to rate how well you know each word. Mark an X next to the correct definition to check your understanding. Then talk with a partner to practice the words.

▲ This **family** is happy.

Key Word	Check Your Understanding	Deepen Your Understanding
① personality (pur-su-**na**-lu-tē) *noun* **Rating: 1 2 3**	☐ how you act and feel ☐ how you run	**Partner 1:** Do these girls show their **personalities**? **Partner 2:** _____ _____
② name (**nām**) *noun* **Rating: 1 2 3**	☐ what a person, place, or thing is called ☐ how old you are	**Partner 2:** What is the **name** of this street? **Partner 1:** _____ _____
③ family (**fam**-lē) *noun* **Rating: 1 2 3**	☐ people in your class ☐ people who are related to you	**Partner 2:** Is this a **family**? **Partner 1:** _____

Vocabulary Workshop

Relate Words

Some words connect, or relate, to each other. When you relate words, you can understand them better.

The **category** tells how the words are related.

Word Web

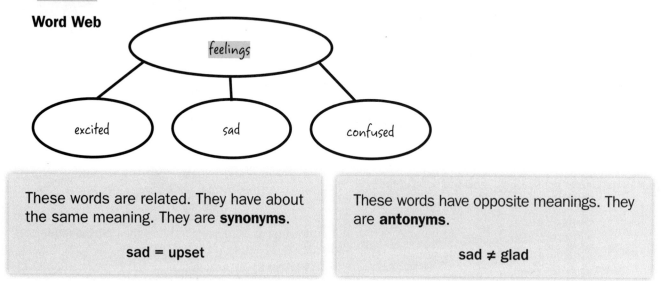

These words are related. They have about the same meaning. They are **synonyms**.

sad = upset

These words have opposite meanings. They are **antonyms**.

sad ≠ glad

Practice Relating Words

A. Read the words in the Word Web below. Add a related word from the box.

Word Web

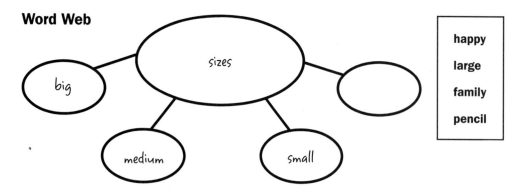

happy

large

family

pencil

B. Read the word pairs. Write = if they are synonyms. Write ≠ if they are antonyms.

1. big _____ small

3. large _____ small

2. big _____ large

4. small _____ little

Put the Strategy to Use

C. Work with a partner. Complete the Word Web. Choose the correct category from the box.

types of weather	words that describe people	parts of the body

Word Web

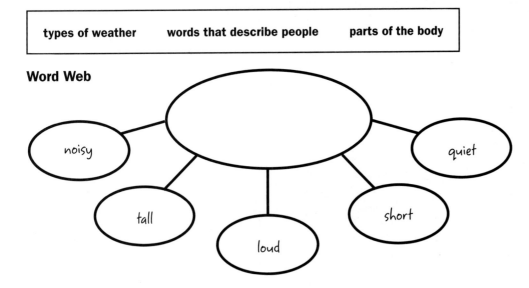

D. Read the paragraph. Cross out the titles that are not good categories for the paragraph. Then circle the two synonyms and underline two antonyms in the paragraph.

> **Food**
>
> **Colors**
>
> **People**
>
> Everyone is different. Some people are *tall*.
> Some people are *short*. Sometimes, people are
> *loud*. But they are not always *noisy*. Sometimes,
> they are quiet.

Prepare to Read

▶ **First Names**
▶ *From* **Romeo and Juliet,** *Act 2, Scene 2*

Key Vocabulary

Circle a number to rate how well you know each word. Mark an *X* next to the correct definition to check your understanding. Then make a drawing to show the meaning of each word.

Rating Scale

1 I do not know this word.	**2** I am not sure of the word's meaning.	**3** I know this word. I can teach the word to someone else.

Key Word	Check Your Understanding	Deepen Your Understanding
❶ call (**cawl**) *verb* Rating: 1 2 3	☐ to use a name for someone or something ☐ to like someone or something	Draw a name tag with the name you **call** your friend.
❷ different (**di**-frunt) *adjective* Rating: 1 2 3	☐ like something else ☐ not like something else	Draw two **different** kinds of fruit.
❸ everyone (**ev**-rē-wun) *pronoun* Rating: 1 2 3	☐ one person in a group ☐ all the people in a group	Draw **everyone** who lives with you.
❹ everywhere (**ev**-rē-wair) *adverb* Rating: 1 2 3	☐ in all places ☐ in one place	Draw a circle with spots **everywhere**.

One orange fish is **unique** next to all the blue fish. ▶

Key Word	Check Your Understanding	Deepen Your Understanding
⑤ friend (**frend**) *noun* Rating: **1 2 3**	☐ a person you care about ☐ a person who works hard	Draw your **friend**.
⑥ like (**līk**) *verb* Rating: **1 2 3**	☐ to look at something ☐ to feel good about something	Draw something dogs **like** to eat.
⑦ other (**u**-thur) *adjective* Rating: **1 2 3**	☐ someone or something else ☐ someone or something you know	Draw a rose and one **other** flower.
⑧ unique (yū-**nēk**) *adjective* Rating: **1 2 3**	☐ the one that is big ☐ the only one of its kind	Draw one **unique** shape and two common shapes.

Before Reading First Names

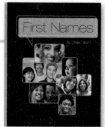

READING STRATEGY: Visualize

HOW TO FORM MENTAL IMAGES

Reading Strategy
Visualize

1. Turn the pages. Look at the pictures.

2. Focus on details. Think about what they make you imagine.

3. Add what you know from your life. Think about people you know.

4. To build your understanding, make a quick drawing. Show what you visualize.

A. Look at the picture. Think about what it makes you imagine.

Look Into the Text

The girls look like _____
_____.
This makes me think about _____
_____.

B. Now draw a picture of what you visualize.

© NGSP & HB

Selection Review First Names

 Who Am I?
Think about your name.

In "First Names," you learned that people's names have different meanings.

Fill in the chart below.

Form a Mental Image	Draw a Picture of What You Visualize
Call our names, and we will answer.	
My name is also the name of a hurricane.	
Surya is the Hindu god of the sun.	
My first name is Kofi. It means "born on Friday."	
But I like my first name. It is unique. I am, too.	

GENRE: Characters in a Play

HOW TO UNDERSTAND CHARACTERS

Actors play the parts of the characters in a play. The names of the characters are in dark type. The words that the characters say come after their names. These words are called dialogue.

1. To identify the characters, find the names.

2. To learn what a character is like, think about what the character says and does.

A. Read the text from the play. Say who the character is.

Look Into the Text

ROMEO. [*to himself*]

Should I wait to hear more or

should I speak?

The character is _____.
He says these words.

B. Now circle the correct word in each sentence to show what you know about the character.

The character speaks to (Juliet/himself). He does not know

what to (do/say). He asks this question because he is not

(sure/happy).

Connect Across Texts
In "First Names," people say what their names mean. Now read an excerpt from a famous play. Romeo and Juliet are in love. What do the characters think a name means?

FROM

ROMEO *and* JULIET

ACT 2, SCENE 2

by William Shakespeare

Romeo and Juliet is a very famous play. William Shakespeare wrote it more than four hundred years ago. But people still read and watch it today.

The play tells a sad story. The Capulet family and the Montague family hate each other. But Juliet Capulet and Romeo Montague fall in love. Do their names make them who they are?

Interact with the Text

1. Characters

Circle the name of the character who speaks first. What question does Juliet ask Romeo?

Juliet asks Romeo why his

name is _____.

2. Characters

Underline the words that tell why Juliet wants Romeo to change his name. Then complete the sentence.

Juliet wants Romeo to

change _____

because her family

_____

_____ .

ACT 2, SCENE 2

JULIET. [*looking down from above*]

Oh, Romeo, Romeo! Why is your name "Romeo Montague"?

Change your name.

Or, just say you love me.

And I will change my name. I will **no longer be** a Capulet.

ROMEO. [*to himself*]

Should I wait to hear more or should I speak?

JULIET. [*continues*]

My family hates the name "Montague."

If you change your name, you will still be the man I love.

What is a name? A rose is a rose

Even if it is not **called** "rose."

And Romeo is Romeo

Even if he is not called "Romeo."

Romeo, give up your name.

If you do,

Then I will give you my heart.

Key Vocabulary
call *verb*, to use a name for someone or something

In Other Words
no longer be stop being

ROMEO. [*looking up at Juliet*]

Your words of love are all I need to hear.

No longer call me "Romeo." Call me "love."

Then I will have a new name and a new life. ❖

Many actors around the world play Juliet.

3. Characters

Who speaks here?

_____

What does Romeo say to Juliet? What do his words tell you? Circle the correct answer. Then complete the sentence.

Romeo tells Juliet to call

him "Romeo" / "love." His

words mean that _____

_____ .

About the Writer

William Shakespeare (1564–1616) is one of England's most famous writers. He wrote poems and plays. His plays are still performed around the world. Many of Shakespeare's plays are now movies, too.

Selection Review *From* Romeo and Juliet, *Act 2, Scene 2*

Romeo and Juliet talk a lot about their names. Think about the words they say. What do their words mean? Work with a partner. Circle the answer you agree with.

What the Character Says	What the Character Means
JULIET. What is a name? A rose is a rose even if it is not called "rose." And Romeo is Romeo even if he is not called "Romeo."	Juliet wants to call Romeo "rose." Juliet thinks names are not important.
JULIET. Romeo, give up your name. If you do, then I will give you my heart.	Juliet (wants/does not want) Romeo to change his name.
ROMEO. No longer call me "Romeo." Call me "love." Then I will have a new name and a new life.	Romeo thinks his name is unique. Romeo will do what Juliet wants.

Reflect and Assess

WRITING: Write About Literature

A. Plan your writing. What do the names in "First Names" relate to? Complete the chart. Then add your name to the chart.

Name	Relates to
Ernesto	
Surya	the Hindu god of the sun
Kofi	
Amy	

B. Read the student model. Then write about your first name. Explain why you have this name.

Student Model

My name is June. I have this name because my birthday is in June. I like my name because I like summer.

Paragraph Organizer

My name is _____

_____.

I have this name because _____

_____.

I like my name because _____

_____.

Integrate the Language Arts

VOCABULARY STUDY: Word Categories

A **word category** is a group of words that go together. The words in a category are often examples. *Amy* is an example of a *name*.

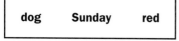

Names
Amy
Ernesto
Surya
Kofi

A. Read each category. Cross out the word that does **not** belong to the category. Then add a word from the box.

| dog | Sunday | red |

1. COLORS: blue, green, friend, _____

2. ANIMALS: cat, apple, fish, _____

3. DAYS OF THE WEEK: Romeo, Monday, Friday, _____

B. Read the words in the box. Then complete the chart. Write each word in the correct category.

| characters | book | desk | teacher | dialogue | play |

School Words	Drama Words

RESEARCH/SPEAKING: Research Name Origins

In "First Names," people say what their names mean. Find out what your name means.

A. Look up your name on the Internet or ask a family member about your name. Use the chart to make notes.

Name	Where It Comes From	What It Means
Clara	Spain	bright

B. Complete the sentences. Use them to tell the group about your name.

My name is _____.

It comes from _____.

It means _____.

I like my name because _____.

> My name is Clara. In Spanish, it means "bright." It is a common name.

Prepare to Read

▶ **Growing Together**
▶ **My People**

Key Vocabulary

Circle a number to rate how well you know each word. Mark an *X* next to the correct definition to check your understanding. Then talk with a partner to practice the words.

Rating Scale

1 I do not know this word.	**2** I am not sure of the word's meaning.	**3** I know this word. I can teach the word to someone else.

Key Word	Check Your Understanding	Deepen Your Understanding
1 beautiful (**byū**-ti-ful) *adjective* Rating: **1 2 3**	☐ pretty, nice to look at ☐ ugly, funny to look at	**Partner 1:** What is a **beautiful** thing to see? **Partner 2:** A **beautiful** thing to see is _____ _____ _____ .
2 grow (**grō**) *verb* Rating: **1 2 3**	☐ to make something you like ☐ to make bigger	**Partner 2:** What is something that can **grow**? **Partner 1:** Something that can **grow** is _____ _____ _____ .
3 hard (**hard**) *adjective* Rating: **1 2 3**	☐ funny ☐ not easy	**Partner 1:** What do you do when your homework is **hard**? **Partner 2:** When my homework is **hard** I _____ _____ _____ .
4 home (**hōm**) *noun* Rating: **1 2 3**	☐ a place where you live ☐ a place where you shop	**Partner 2:** Where is your **home**? **Partner 1:** My **home** is in _____ _____ _____ .

We **wait** for the fruit to **grow**. ▶

Key Word	Check Your Understanding	Deepen Your Understanding
5 leave (lēv) *verb* Rating: 1 2 3	☐ to come back ☐ to go away	**Partner 1:** What do you do when you **leave** school? **Partner 2:** When I **leave** school I _____ _____ _____ .
6 miss (mis) *verb* Rating: 1 2 3	☐ to be sad someone is not with you ☐ to be sad someone is not a friend	**Partner 2:** How do you feel when you **miss** someone? **Partner 1:** When I **miss** someone I feel _____ _____ _____ .
7 together (tu-**ge**-thur) *adverb* Rating: 1 2 3	☐ far way from each other ☐ combined with each other	**Partner 1:** What happens if you mix red and yellow **together**? **Partner 2:** If you mix red and yellow **together** you make _____ .
8 wait (wāt) *verb* Rating: 1 2 3	☐ to stay in one place until something happens ☐ to be sad until something happens	**Partner 2:** What is something you can **wait** for? **Partner 1:** You can **wait** for _____ _____ _____ .

Before Reading Growing Together

READING STRATEGY: Visualize

Reading Strategy
Visualize

HOW TO FORM MENTAL IMAGES

1. Look for details. Find words that tell how things look, sound, smell, taste, and feel.

2. Picture the place. Ask, "What does it look like?"

3. Make a quick drawing. Show how you see the place in your mind.

A. Read the text. Circle words that tell how things look, sound, smell, taste, or feel. Then picture the place.

Look Into the Text

It is hard to leave a home. It is even harder to make a new home. Everything is new. Everything is strange. Everything is different.

The writer says that the place is _____.
This makes me picture _____
_____
_____.

B. Now draw a picture of your mental image.

Selection Review Growing Together

 Who Am I?
Learn how your family and culture are part of you.

In "Growing Together," you read about a girl who learns to live in two different cultures.

A. Read the passages. Then circle words that help you understand how things look, smell, sound, taste, and feel.

I tell Papi how I feel. "I hate it here! I am not like them. They are not like me!"	"You take a branch from one tree. You add it to another tree. Then they grow together."	I am a tree. I grow both mangoes and magnolias.

B. Now draw how you see each passage in your mind.

Before Reading My People

ELEMENTS OF POETRY: Patterns

How to READ POETRY

1. Read the poem aloud. Ask, "How does it sound?"

2. Read the poem again slowly. Look for patterns, or parts that are repeated. Listen for patterns.

3. Ask, "What does the pattern help me understand or feel?"

4. Read the poem again. Write your ideas on a self-stick note.

A. Read the lines of the poem aloud. Look and listen for a pattern. Then complete the sentence in the thought bubble.

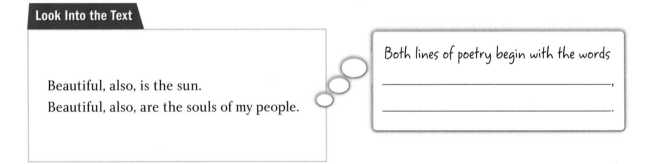

Look Into the Text

Beautiful, also, is the sun.
Beautiful, also, are the souls of my people.

Both lines of poetry begin with the words

_____,

_____.

B. Now complete the self-stick note. Explain what the pattern helps you understand.

The souls of the people are like _____

_____

_____.

They are both _____

_____

_____.

Connect Across Texts

In "Growing Together," Carmita explains how she is part of two cultures. What does the speaker in this poem say about the people in his culture?

My People

by
Langston Hughes

Illustrated by
Sara Tyson

Interact with the Text

1. Patterns in Poetry

Circle the words in the poem that are about things in nature.

What does the speaker say about these things?

The speaker says they are

all _____.

Why are they important?

They are important because

_____.

The night is beautiful,
So the faces of my people.

The stars are beautiful,
So the eyes of my people.

Beautiful, also, is the sun.
Beautiful, also, are the souls of my people.

About the Poet

Langston Hughes (1902–1967) was a famous American writer. He was an important person in the Harlem Renaissance. During this time, Americans celebrated African American culture in art, writing, music, and dance.

Selection Review My People

Reread "My People." Think about what the words mean. Share your ideas with a partner. Complete the chart.

What the Speaker Says	What the Words Mean
The night is beautiful, So the faces of my people.	Night is dark. The speaker means that the people are dark like the night.
The stars are beautiful, So the eyes of my people.	Stars are _____. The people's _____ are _____ like stars.
Beautiful, also, is the sun. Beautiful, also, are the souls of my people.	The sun is _____. The people's _____ are _____ like the sun.

WRITING: Write About Literature

A. Draw a picture of yourself in a place that is important to you. Include two family members in your picture. Label each person in your drawing.

Person 1: _____   Me   **Person 2:** _____

B. Finish the caption to give more information about the picture. Use the student model as a guide.

Student Model

This place is my aunt's home in Mexico. It is important to me because we go there every summer. The people are my cousin Rita and my Aunt Carmen.

Organizer

This place is _____ .

It is important to me because _____

_____ . The people in this picture are _____

_____ and _____ .

Integrate the Language Arts

VOCABULARY STUDY: Concept Clusters

A **Concept Cluster** shows information about a certain word or an idea.
Look at this Concept Cluster for *Georgia*.

Concept Cluster

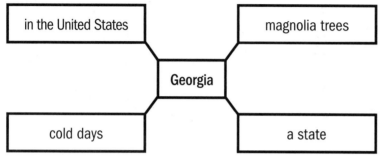

in the United States		magnolia trees
	Georgia	
cold days		a state

A. Complete these sentences about your home.

1. My home is in _____.

2. _____ lives there.

3. My favorite place at home is _____.

4. My home is _____.

B. Use words from the box to make a Concept Cluster for the word *home*.

family	everywhere	noisy	the kitchen	my bedroom	United States	quiet	medium

Concept Cluster

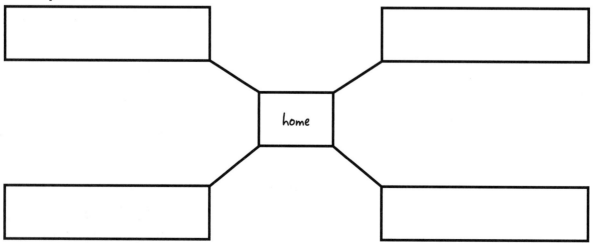

home

© NGSP & HB

COMPREHENSION: Sequence

The things that happen in a story are the events. The order in which they happen is the sequence. Here are two events that happen in the story:

"Growing Together"
1. Carmita thinks about living in Cuba.
2. She tells her father how she feels.

A. Reread "Growing Together." Answer the questions.

1. What does Carmita think about? _____

_____

2. What does Carmita tell her father? _____

_____

3. What does Carmita's father tell her? _____

_____

4. What does Carmita learn about being a Cuban living in the United States? _____

_____

_____

B. Now complete the chart below. Number the events to show the correct sequence.

"Growing Together"

Sequence	Event
	Carmita understands she must wait.
	Carmita's father says she is the mango tree and Georgia is the magnolia.
6	Carmita says she is an American.
1	Carmita thinks about living in Cuba.
2	Carmita tells her father how she feels.
	Carmita's father tells her what it means to graft a tree.

Prepare to Read

▶ **Ways to Know You**
▶ **Who Is She?**

Key Vocabulary

Circle a number to rate how well you know each word. Mark an X next to the correct definition to check your understanding. Then create a drawing to show the meaning of each word.

Rating Scale

1 I do not know this word.	**2** I am not sure of the word's meaning.	**3** I know this word. I can teach the word to someone else.

Key Word	Check Your Understanding	Deepen Your Understanding
❶ find (**fīnd**)　*verb* Rating: 1　2　3	☐ to ask where something is ☐ to learn where something is	Draw something you can **find** in your bag.
❷ idea (ī-**dē**-u)　*noun* Rating: 1　2　3	☐ a song or a poem ☐ a thought or a plan	Draw an **idea** for a new kind of car.
❸ no one (**nō**-wun)　*pronoun* Rating: 1　2　3	☐ no person ☐ many people	Draw a food **no one** likes to eat.
❹ pattern (**pa**-turn)　*noun* Rating: 1　2　3	☐ a kind of food ☐ a design that repeats	Draw a **pattern** with X and O.

This **scientist studies** cells. What will she **find**? ▶

Key Word	Check Your Understanding	Deepen Your Understanding
5 **scientist** (**sī**-un-tist) *noun* Rating: 1 2 3	☐ a person who studies the things in our world ☐ a person who works in a store	Draw something a **scientist** uses at work.
6 **similar** (**si**-mu-lur) *adjective* Rating: 1 2 3	☐ very different ☐ almost the same	Draw two **similar** fruits.
7 **special** (**spe**-shul) *adjective* Rating: 1 2 3	☐ not like other things ☐ exactly like other things	Draw something you wear that is **special**.
8 **study** (**stu**-dē) *verb* Rating: 1 2 3	☐ to bring something with you ☐ to look at something carefully	Draw something you can use to **study** the stars.

Before Reading Ways to Know You

READING STRATEGY: Visualize

Reading Strategy
Visualize

HOW TO FORM MENTAL IMAGES

1. Look first at the pictures. What pictures do you form in your own mind?

2. As you read, look for words that describe people, places, and events. Use those words to form more pictures in your mind.

3. Ask, "What do the pictures mean?" Use the pictures to help you understand the text.

4. Write your ideas on self-stick notes.

A. Read the text. Look at the picture. Think about what it means to you. Then complete the thought bubble.

Look Into the Text

Fingerprint Patterns

Whorl   Loop   Arch

The picture shows _____

_____ .

In my mind I see _____

_____

_____ .

B. Now complete the self-stick note. Explain how the picture helped you understand the text.

From the picture and the text, I know that the words "Whorl," "Loop," and "Arch" are names for _____

_____

_____ .

Selection Review Ways to Know You

 Who Am I?
Discover how your body is unique.

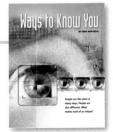

In "Ways to Know You," you read about ways that your body is unique. Think about what you learned from the pictures and the text. Fill in the missing notes.

Section Head	What the Pictures Show	What I Learned
Fingerprints	The pictures show triplets and 3 kinds of _____ _____ _____ _____.	Each fingerprint is _____. There are _____ kinds of fingerprint _____. They are called "whorl," _____ and _____.
Eyes	The pictures show eyes that have different shapes and _____. I also see 2 parts of the eye: the _____ and the _____ _____.	Eyes look similar but they have _____ _____. The iris is unique in more than _____ different ways. Everyone's retina has a different _____.
DNA	The pictures show a girl with curly hair. I also see a piece of _____ _____ _____.	DNA is your body's unique _____. It is _____ in your body. The girl's hair is curly because of _____. The _____ of each person's DNA is _____.

Before Reading Who Is She?

TEXT STRUCTURE: Sequence

HOW TO IDENTIFY SEQUENCE

1. Read the text. Think about the **sequence**, or order, of events.

2. Write the events in a **Sequence Chart**.

3. Then use your chart to identify what happened first, next, and last.

A. Read the text. Think about the sequence of events.

Look Into the Text

Dr. John Daugman had an idea. He looked at the picture of the girl. He studied her eyes. He found their special pattern. Then he studied a picture of the woman. The pattern was the same.

B. Now complete the Sequence Chart.

Sequence Chart

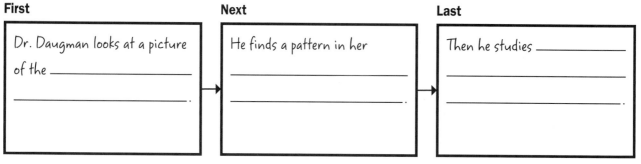

First	Next	Last
Dr. Daugman looks at a picture of the _____ _____.	He finds a pattern in her _____ _____.	Then he studies _____ _____.

Who Is She?

by Joan Johnson

A picture of this girl was in a magazine in 1985. But **no one** knew the girl's name. Years later, people wanted to **find** her. They wanted to know who she was. They looked in many places.

Interact with the Text

1. Sequence
In which year did this girl appear in a magazine? Circle the answer.

Find two other words in the text that tell about time. Circle them.

Key Vocabulary
special *adjective*, not like others, unique
no one *pronoun*, no person, nobody
find *verb*, to learn where a person or thing is

2. Sequence

Complete the Sequence Chart.

Sequence Chart

First

Picture of girl is in magazine in 1985.

↓

Next

↓

Last

In _____, people

find _____.

3. Sequence

Now look at the pictures. Which picture is from 1985? Which picture is from 2002? Write the answers.

This picture is from _____.   This picture is from _____.

In 2002, they found her. How did
they know she was the same person?
They asked a **scientist**.

Key Vocabulary

scientist *noun*, person who studies
how things work

Dr. John Daugman had an **idea**. He looked at the picture of the girl. He **studied** her eyes. He found their special **pattern**. Then he studied a picture of the woman. The pattern was the same.

Interact with the Text

4. Sequence

What happened after people found the girl? Complete the sentence.

A scientist named _____

studied patterns of _____
to see if the girl and the
woman are _____
.

Key Vocabulary

idea *noun*, thought, plan

study *verb*, to look at something carefully

pattern *noun*, a design that repeats

5. Sequence

What happened last? Complete the sentence.

The scientist found that the two pictures show

_____

_____ .

Her name is Sharbat Gula.

She is from **Afghanistan**.

She is the girl in the picture. ❖

In Other Words
Afghanistan a country in southern Asia

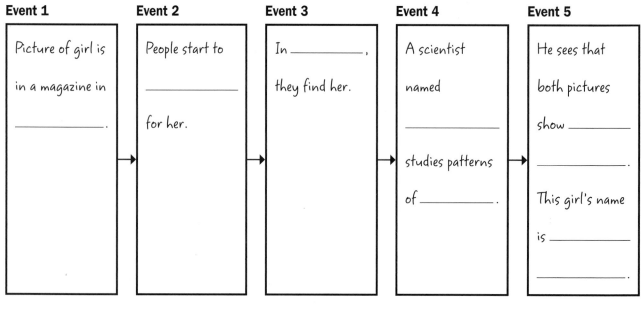

Selection Review Who Is She?

Think about the events in this magazine article. Complete the Sequence Chart.

Sequence Chart

Event 1	Event 2	Event 3	Event 4	Event 5
Picture of girl is in a magazine in _____ .	People start to _____ for her.	In _____, they find her.	A scientist named _____ studies patterns of _____ .	He sees that both pictures show _____ _____ . This girl's name is _____ .

Reflect and Assess

WRITING: Write About Literature

A. Plan your writing. Complete the chart. Write the names of people you know. Then write notes to explain how each person is unique, or special.

Person	How the Person Is Unique or Special
my mother	speaks three languages

B. Read the student model. Then complete the paragraph. Write two ways people are unique, or special.

Student Model

> Our body patterns make us special. But we are special in other ways, too. For example, people speak different languages.

Paragraph Organizer

Our body patterns make us special. But we are special in other ways, too. For example, _____

_____

_____

_____.

Another example of something that makes us unique is _____

_____

_____

_____.

Integrate the Language Arts

VOCABULARY STUDY: Synonyms and Antonyms

Synonyms are words with similar meanings.

beautiful = pretty

Antonyms are words with opposite meanings.

beautiful ≠ ugly

A. Read the words. Match the synonyms.

___ **1.** pattern   **a.** special

___ **2.** picture   **b.** photo

___ **3.** no one   **c.** design

___ **4.** unique   **d.** nobody

B. Read the words. Match the antonyms.

___ **5.** similar   **e.** everyone

___ **6.** no one   **f.** lose

___ **7.** find   **g.** different

___ **8.** many   **h.** few

COMPREHENSION: Make a Time Line

A time line shows dates and events in the order they happened.

A. Reread "Who Is She?" Look at the time line at the bottom of the page.
Then write the missing information.

1. When was the picture of the girl in a magazine? _____

2. What year did they find the person in the picture? _____

3. What did Dr. Daugman study before he knew she was the same person?

   He studied _____.

4. What did Dr. Daugman do next?

   He _____

   _____

   _____.

B. Use your answers from Part A to complete the sentences in the time line.

Time Line

First   People find _____. They take her picture.

Next   Dr. John Daugman studies her _____.

Last   He finds that both pictures are of

_____.

A picture of a girl
is in a magazine.

1985   2002

Vocabulary Review

A. Study each picture. Circle the word that completes each sentence.

1.

The two shoes are **(hard / different)**.
They are not the same.

2.

The people **(wait / grow)** for a
bus to arrive.

3.

A person who studies how things work
is a **(pattern / scientist)**.

4.
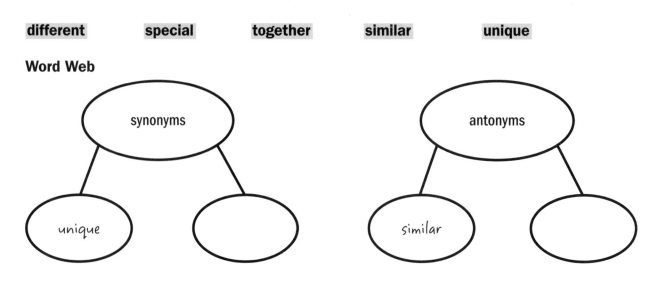

A **(friend / home)** is where you live.

B. Choose words to complete the Word Webs below.

different　　special　　together　　similar　　unique

Word Web

synonyms

unique

antonyms

similar

Unit 1 Vocabulary

beautiful	family	home	name	scientist	unique
call	find	idea	no one	similar	wait
different	friend	leave	other	special	
everyone	grow	like	pattern	study	
everywhere	hard	miss	personality	together	

C. Read each sentence. Circle the word that completes each sentence correctly.

1. My (**friend / pattern**) and I play video games a lot.

2. An apple does not look (**similar / beautiful**) to a banana.

3. My (**personality / home**) is the red house.

4. When I (**name / study**) I get good grades.

5. I water my plant. I want it to (**grow / leave**) tall.

6. My grandfather lives far away. I (**find / miss**) him.

7. I (**call / wait**) my mother every day.

8. Her room is a mess. Books are (**everywhere / together**)!

9. The mother, the father, and the two children are a (**name / family**).

10. Learning to play the guitar is (**other / hard**). I practice a lot.

11. (**Everyone / No one**) likes the nice teacher.

Unit Vocabulary

Circle a number to rate how well you know each word. Mark an *X* next to the correct definition to check your understanding. Then talk with a partner to practice the words.

▲ The girl gets **advice** from her friends.

Key Word	Check Your Understanding	Deepen Your Understanding
1 advice (ud-**vīs**) *noun* Rating: 1 2 3	☐ a food that you like ☐ an idea about what someone should do	Partner 1: Do the friends give **advice**? Partner 2: _____ _____
2 learn (**lurn**) *verb* Rating: 1 2 3	☐ to buy a new thing ☐ to understand a new thing	Partner 2: Do they **learn** about cats? Partner 1: _____ _____
3 wisdom (**wiz**-dum) *noun* Rating: 1 2 3	☐ what you learn over time ☐ what you can eat	Partner 1: Does he have **wisdom**? Partner 2: _____ _____

Vocabulary Workshop

Use Word Parts

Sometimes you can join two smaller words to form a **compound word**. Put the meanings of the smaller words together to understand the whole word. Complete the sentence in the thought bubble.

compound word

news + paper = newspaper

A newspaper is a _____ that gives news.

Some words are made up of a **base word** and a **suffix**. A suffix is added to the end of the base word. It changes the word's meaning.

base word | suffix

loud + -ly = loudly

The ending **-ly** means "in that way." So **loudly** means "in a _____ way."

Practice Using Word Parts

Read the text. Circle the word parts in each underlined word. Think about what the word means. Then complete the chart.

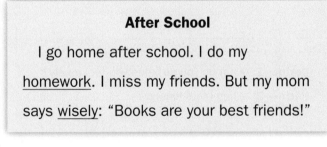

After School

I go home after school. I do my homework. I miss my friends. But my mom says wisely: "Books are your best friends!"

Word	Word Parts	Meaning
homework	home _____	work done at _____
wisely	_____ _____	in a _____ way

Put the Strategy to Use

Work with a partner. Use what you know about word parts to figure out the meaning of each underlined word. Write the meaning.

1. People use their time differently. (in a _____ way)

2. My friends and I play football. (a game that uses a _____ and a _____)

3. My best friend also plays the piano beautifully. (_____)

Prepare to Read

▶ How Ananse Gave Wisdom to the World
▶ Good Advice from Teens

Key Vocabulary

Circle a number to rate how well you know each word. Mark an *X* next to the correct definition to check your understanding. Then talk with a partner to practice each word.

Rating Scale

| 1 | I do not know this word. | 2 | I am not sure of the word's meaning. | 3 | I know this word. I can teach the word to someone else. |

Key Word	Check Your Understanding	Deepen Your Understanding
1 angry (**ang**-grē) *adjective* Rating: 1 2 3	☐ pleased, happy ☐ mad, upset	**Partner 1:** When are you **angry**? **Partner 2:** I am **angry** when _____ _____ _____ .
2 difficult (**di**-fi-kult) *adjective* Rating: 1 2 3	☐ the same ☐ hard to do	**Partner 2:** What is **difficult** for you to do? **Partner 1:** _____ is **difficult** for me.
3 lonely (**lōn**-lē) *adjective* Rating: 1 2 3	☐ sad and by yourself ☐ happy and special	**Partner 1:** What do you do when you feel **lonely**? **Partner 2:** When I feel **lonely**, I _____ _____ _____ .
4 problem (**prah**-blum) *noun* Rating: 1 2 3	☐ something beautiful ☐ something you need to fix	**Partner 2:** When can a car have a **problem**? **Partner 1:** A car can have a **problem** when it _____ _____ _____ .

Selfish people can make other people **angry**. ▶

Key Word	Check Your Understanding	Deepen Your Understanding
5 selfish (**sel**-fish) *adjective* **Rating: 1 2 3**	☐ caring about everyone ☐ caring only about yourself	**Partner 1:** What do **selfish** people do? **Partner 2: Selfish** people _____ _____ _____ .
6 share (**shair**) *verb* **Rating: 1 2 3**	☐ to like other people ☐ to give to other people	**Partner 2:** Do you usually **share** your lunch? **Partner 1:** _____ , I usually (**share**/do not **share**) my lunch because _____ _____ _____ .
7 simple (**sim**-pul) *adjective* **Rating: 1 2 3**	☐ easy ☐ beautiful	**Partner 1:** What is an example of a **simple** math problem? **Partner 2:** An example of a **simple** math problem is: _____ .
8 solution (su-**lü**-shun) *noun* **Rating: 1 2 3**	☐ an answer ☐ a pattern	**Partner 2:** What is the **solution** for 5+5? **Partner 1:** The **solution** is _____ .

Before Reading How Ananse Gave Wisdom to the World

READING STRATEGY: Ask Questions

HOW TO ASK QUESTIONS

1. Look at the pictures. Ask yourself questions about the pictures.

2. Ask questions that begin with words like *Who, What, When,* and *Where*. Write your questions on self-stick notes.

3. Read the text to find the answers.

A. Look at the picture. Write questions about it on the self-stick notes.

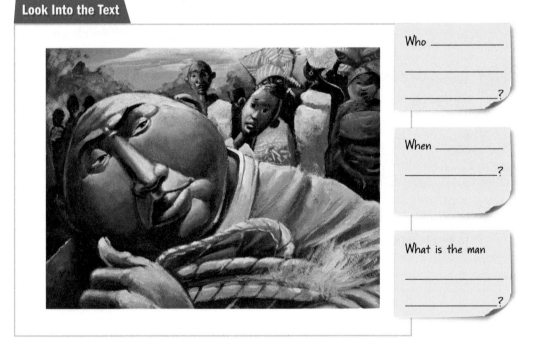

Look Into the Text

Who _____
_____
_____?

When _____
_____?

What is the man
_____
_____?

> Long ago, there lived a man called Kwaku Ananse. He lived with his wife and his son. His son's name was Ntikuma.

B. Now read the text to find the answers to your questions. Complete the sentences about the picture.

The main person in the picture is _____. Other people in the picture may include _____. The story happens _____.

Selection Review How Ananse Gave Wisdom to the World

EQ **What Makes Us Wise?**
Find out how taking good advice makes us wise.

In "How Ananse Gave Wisdom to the World," you learned that good advice can come from anyone. Complete the chart. It shows a question for each picture.

Picture	Question	Answer
	Who are the people in the picture?	They are Ananse, Ntikuma, and Ananse's neighbors.
	_____ is in the pot?	_____ is in the pot.
	_____ is Ananse?	He is _____.
	Why is it difficult for Ananse to climb the tree?	He cannot hold the _____ _____.
	_____ does Ntikuma tell his father?	He tells his father to put the pot _____ _____.
	_____ happens to the pot and the wisdom?	The pot _____. The wisdom _____ _____.

TEXT STRUCTURE: Problem and Solution

HOW TO RECOGNIZE TEXT STRUCTURE

1. Read the title and text. What is the text about? How do you know? Look for a problem that the writer wants you to know about. Then look for text that gives solutions.

2. As you read, think about how the writer organizes the ideas.

3. Make a chart to connect problems and solutions.

A. Read the text. Think about the text structure of this Advice Forum. Complete each sentence in the thought bubble.

Look Into the Text

Advice Forum
Post
AndyBird's Question: I just started high school . . . I feel so lonely. No one talks to me. What can I do?
Friendly's Answer: Join other students.
Rosa's Answer: Introduce yourself to other students.

> The word "question" is a clue. This text describes a _____.
> The word "answer" is a clue.
> Each answer gives a different
> _____.

B. Now complete the chart.

Problem-and-Solution Chart

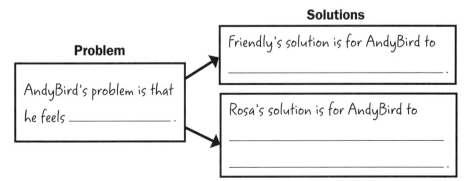

Problem

AndyBird's problem is that he feels _____.

Solutions

Friendly's solution is for AndyBird to _____.

Rosa's solution is for AndyBird to _____.

Good Advice from Teens

Connect Across Texts

In "How Ananse Gave Wisdom to the World," Ananse hears wisdom from his son. How is wisdom **shared** in this web forum?

Advice Forum

Author	Post
 **AndyBird**	**AndyBird's Question:** I just started high school. I'm in grade nine. I moved from another school. Everyone knows each other. I feel so **lonely**. No one talks to me. What can I do?
 **Friendly**	**Friendly's Answer: Join** other students. Talk about a class you have together. Try joining **a club**. It's a good way to meet people. **Be yourself. Be confident**. I hope **all goes well**.

Key Vocabulary

share *verb*, to give part of something to others

lonely *adjective*, sad because you are not with other people

In Other Words

Join Meet

a club a group that does things together

Be yourself. Be confident. Know that you are a good person.

all goes well you will be happy

Interact with the Text

2. Problem and Solution

Who are the two authors on this page?

_____

_____

Do they give advice or tell about a problem?

_____

_____

Author	Post
Rosa	**Rosa's Answer: Introduce yourself** to other students. Talk to a teacher or **counselor**. Ask them about ways to meet people. **Relax**. Go slowly. You will find some great friends.
Griffen	**Griffen's Answer:** Sports! Find a sport you like to play. **It never fails**. Join a school club. Sit with a few **strangers** at lunch.

In Other Words
Introduce yourself Say "hello"
counselor someone who can give you advice
Relax. Don't worry.
It never fails. Playing sports always helps.
strangers people you do not know

Selection Review   Good Advice from Teens

Think about the ideas in this Web forum. Complete the chart.

Problem-and-Solution Chart

Solutions

Solution 1 (Friendly)

Talk to _____

or _____ .

Problem

AndyBird

I feel _____ .

Solution 2 (_____)

Talk to a _____ .

Ask them about _____

_____ .

Solution 3 (Griffen)

Play _____ , or sit with

_____ at lunch.

Reflect and Assess

WRITING: Write About Literature

A. Plan your writing. Reread "Good Advice from Teens." Think of your own solution to AndyBird's problem. Add it to the chart.

> 1. **Describe AndyBird's problem.**
>   AndyBird feels lonely and wants to make friends.

> 2. **Write the solution.**
>   AndyBird can _____
>   _____ .

> 3. **Explain why your solution works.**
>   He will _____
>   _____ .

B. Now write a paragraph to explain your solution to AndyBird's problem.

Paragraph Organizer

AndyBird is in grade _____ . He just moved from _____

_____ . He feels _____ because _____

_____ . AndyBird should _____

_____ . This will help him make friends because he will _____

_____ .

Integrate the Language Arts

VOCABULARY STUDY: Compound Words

A compound word is made up of two smaller words. To read a compound word:

- Break it into parts.
- Think about the meaning of each part.
- Put the meanings together to understand the whole word.

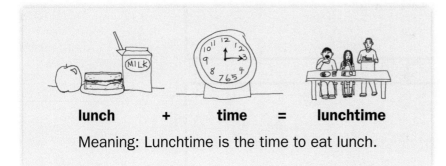

lunch   +   time   =   lunchtime

Meaning: Lunchtime is the time to eat lunch.

A. Find the meaning of each underlined word. Make a drawing of each word part if it helps.

1. I go to the library every <u>afternoon</u>. Meaning: _____

2. Today, a new librarian gives me a <u>paperback</u> book. Meaning: _____

3. Her <u>nametag</u> says: "Rita." Meaning: _____

4. She puts books on a <u>bookshelf</u>. Meaning: _____

B. Read the compound words in the box. Think about the word parts.
Choose the right word to complete each sentence.

grandfather	bookmark	eyelids	bedroom

5. My _____ often comes to the library to read with me.

6. When he gets tired of reading, his _____ close.

7. He puts a _____ in his book to note the page.

8. I tell him, "Grandfather, don't sleep in the library! Sleep in your _____."

COMPREHENSION: Describe Characters

Characters are the people or animals that a story is about. When you describe characters, you tell about what they are like. To learn what characters are like, look at their actions, or what they do.

A. Review "How Ananse Gave Wisdom to the World." Then answer the questions.

1. What does Ntikuma do to help his father?

He tells him to _____ .

What does this show about what Ntikuma is like?

It shows that he is _____ .

2. What does Ananse do after Ntikuma gives him advice?

He gets _____

and _____ .

What does this show about what Ananse is like?

It shows that he gets _____ easily.

B. Now use your answers to complete the Character Chart.

Character Chart

Character	The Character's Actions	What the Actions Show About the Character
Ananse	wants to keep all the wisdom for himself	is selfish; greedy
	gets _____ and throws down the _____	
Ntikuma	follows his father into the forest	is curious; wants to know things
	tells his father to _____	

C. Describe Ananse or Ntikuma to a partner. Use your chart to help you.

Prepare to Read

▶ *From* **Be Water, My Friend: The Early Years of Bruce Lee**
▶ **Hands**

Key Vocabulary

Circle a number to rate how well you know each word. Mark an *X* next to the correct definition to check your understanding. Then complete the sentences.

Rating Scale

1 I do not know this word.	**2** I am not sure of the word's meaning.	**3** I know this word. I can teach the word to someone else.

Key Word	Check Your Understanding	Deepen Your Understanding
1 break (**brāk**) *verb* Rating: 1 2 3	☐ to separate into pieces ☐ to put together	You can **break** glass with a _____ _____ _____ .
2 explain (**ik-splān**) *verb* Rating: 1 2 3	☐ to make something clear ☐ to make something difficult	When you **explain** a word you _____ _____ _____ .
3 fight (**fīt**) *verb* Rating: 1 2 3	☐ to hurt or yell at someone ☐ to study for a long time	When you **fight**, you feel _____ _____ _____ .
4 harm (**harm**) *verb* Rating: 1 2 3	☐ to hurt ☐ to cry	You can **harm** your eyes if you _____ _____ _____ .

A teacher can **explain** and help us **understand** new things. ▶

Key Word	Check Your Understanding	Deepen Your Understanding
5 **rest** (**rest**) *verb* Rating: 1 2 3	☐ to stop ☐ to work	I **rest** when I _____ _____ _____.
6 **touch** (**tuch**) *verb* Rating: 1 2 3	☐ to think ☐ to feel	Do not **touch** _____ _____ _____.
7 **tough** (**tuf**) *adjective* Rating: 1 2 3	☐ angry ☐ strong	Athletes are **tough** because _____ _____ _____.
8 **understand** (un-dur-**stand**) *verb* Rating: 1 2 3	☐ to know what something means ☐ to take something away	When I do not **understand** a word, I _____ _____ _____.

Before Reading *from* Be Water, My Friend

READING STRATEGY: Ask Questions

Reading Strategy
Ask Questions

HOW TO ASK QUESTIONS

1. Stop and think about the text as you read. Ask yourself questions about it.

2. Ask questions that begin with words like *Who, What, When, Where,* and *Why.* Write your questions on self-stick notes.

3. To find the answers, reread the text or read on.

A. Read the text. Then read the question on the self-stick note. Do you have to reread or read on to find the answer?

Look Into the Text

"How can I be gentle while I am fighting?" Bruce asked.

Yip Man told Bruce to think about it.

Bruce went out in his boat. He started to think. Gentleness? It didn't make sense. He did not understand. He got angry. He hit the water.

Bruce hit the water again. It didn't break. It ran through his hands. Water was soft. But it could also break through anything in the world.

Bruce returned to Yip Man. "Gentleness," he said. "I think I understand."

Why does Bruce get angry?

I _____ to find the answer.

B. Ask another question about the text. Write it on the blue self-stick note.

Now write the answer to your question.

_____

Did you reread or read on to find the answer?

I _____ to find the answer.

Selection Review *from* Be Water, My Friend

EQ **What Makes Us Wise?**
Think about the wisdom of elders and mentors.

In "Be Water, My Friend," you learned how Bruce Lee got good advice from a teacher. Complete the chart. Reread the text if you need to.

Question	Answer
Who was Bruce Lee?	He was a famous kung fu student and teacher.
Why did his family call him Mo Si Tung?	Mo Si Tung means _____. Bruce was always _____.
Who was Yip Man?	He was _____
Why was Yip Man unhappy?	He was unhappy because _____
_____ did Yip Man say about martial arts?	He said that martial arts are _____
_____ did Bruce go out in his boat?	He went out _____
_____ did Bruce hit the water?	He hit the water because he was _____.
_____ did Bruce notice about the water?	He noticed that water is both _____ and _____.
_____ did Bruce do to beat a big opponent?	He _____.
_____ did Bruce say to himself, "Be water, my friend"?	He was telling himself to _____

Before Reading Hands

Story Elements: Character

> ### HOW TO ANALYZE CHARACTERS
>
> **1.** Read the text.
>
> **2.** Write what the character looks like. Write what the character does.
>
> **3.** Read your notes. Think about similar people. Then decide what the character is like.

A. Read the text. Think about the character Uhmma.

Look Into the Text

Uhmma said her hands were her life. But she only wished to see our hands holding books. You must use this, she said. She pointed to her head.

B. The text does not tell you what Uhmma looks like. Write what you think she looks like. Complete the Character Chart.

Character Chart

Character	What Character Looks Like	What Character Does	What Character Is Like
Uhmma	_____ _____ _____ _____ _____ _____	She tells her children to _____ _____ _____ _____ _____.	She is someone who cares about _____ _____ _____ _____ _____.

Connect Across Texts

In the selection from "Be Water, My Friend," Bruce Lee learns that martial arts aren't always used to **harm** *others. In this short story, Young Ju learns something important from her mother.*

H A N D S

by An Na

Uhmma's hands are as old as **sand**. In the mornings, they **scratched** across our faces. Wake up. Time for school.

At work, her hands **sewed** hundreds of **jeans**. They knew how to make a meal in ten minutes for hungry **customers**.

At home, they washed our dishes. They cleaned the floor. Uhmma's hands rarely **rested**.

Interact with the Text

1. Character
Underline the text that tells what Uhmma does at work and at home. Then complete the sentences below.

At work, Uhmma
_____
_____ .

At home, Uhmma
_____
_____ .

What does this tell you about Uhmma?

Uhmma is someone who
_____
_____
_____
_____
_____ .

Key Vocabulary
harm *verb*, to hurt
rest *verb*, to not work

In Other Words
Uhmma's Mom's (in Korean)
sand the earth
scratched moved with a rough feeling
sewed made
jeans pants
customers people at a restaurant

2. Character

Underline a sentence that tells something Uhmma does with her children.

But sometimes her hands opened. **Palms** up. A flower finally open to the bees.

My brother Joon and I sat on either side of her. She read stories in the lines of our palms.

Look, Young Ju, Uhmma said. Your intelligence line is strong. Maybe you will become a doctor. Uhmma **touched** the line. It **tickled**.

Joon **pushed** away my hand. Look at my intelligence line, Uhmma.

These baby hands have lines? Let me see, Uhmma said. She studied it for a moment. Then she kissed the middle. Plop. A raindrop on water. Joon **giggled**.

We were always reaching to touch Uhmma's **sandpaper** palms.

Key Vocabulary
touch _verb_, to feel

In Other Words
Palms Insides
tickled made me laugh
pushed moved
giggled laughed
sandpaper rough

Uhmma said her hands were her life. But she only wished
to see our hands holding books. You must use this, she
said. She pointed to her head.

I walk with Uhmma now. Her hand is held in mine.

I study these lines **of her past**. I want to remove the
scars. I want to fill in the **cracks** in the skin. I **envelop**
Uhmma's hands in my own soft palms. Close them together.
Like a book. A **Siamese prayer**. I tell her, I want to **erase**
these scars for you.

In Other Words
of her past that tell about her life
scars hurt places
cracks signs of hard work
envelop hold
Siamese prayer special wish
erase take away

4. Character
Circle the words that
tell what Uhmma's
hands look like. How
did her hands get
this way?

_____

_____

_____

_____

_____

5. Character

What does Uhmma say to Young Ju? Underline the text. What does she mean?

She means that

_____

_____

_____

_____ .

Uhmma gently **slips** her hands from mine. She **stares** for a moment at her tough skin. Then she speaks **firmly**. These are my hands, Young Ju. Uhmma puts her arm around **my waist**. We continue our walk along the beach.

Key Vocabulary
tough *adjective*, strong, not easily hurt

In Other Words
slips takes
stares looks hard
firmly with a strong voice
my waist the middle of my body

Selection Review Hands

Reread "Hands." Talk with a partner about Uhmma. What is she like? Complete the Character Chart with details about Uhmma.

Character Chart

Character	What Character Looks Like	What Character Does	What Character Is Like
Uhmma	Her hands are like sand. They _____ _____ _____ _____ . I think she looks _____ _____ _____ _____ .	She wakes up her children, _____ _____ _____ _____ _____ .	She is someone who works hard, _____ _____ _____ _____ .

Reflect and Assess

WRITING: Write About Literature

A. Plan your writing. Find these quotations in the selections. Complete the chart.

Quotation	Who Says It? To Whom?	What Does It Mean?
"Heavy snow sometimes breaks big branches. But smaller plants that look weak bend and survive."	Yip Man says this to Bruce Lee.	_____ _____ _____
"You must use this, she said. She pointed to her head."	_____ says this to _____ .	_____ _____

B. Read the example. Then choose a quotation from the chart. Explain how you use it in your life.

Student Model

> Quotation: "You must use this, she said. She pointed to her head."
>
> The quotation means that it is important to use your mind.
> In my life, I try to use my mind to study. I also try to use my
> mind to think about problems and find solutions.

Organizer

Quotation: _____

The quotation means _____

_____ .

In my life, I try to _____

_____ .

I also try to _____

_____ .

Integrate the Language Arts

VOCABULARY STUDY: Suffixes

A suffix is a word part added to the end of a word. The suffix *-ly* means "in that way." See how it changes the meaning of the words in the chart.

WORD	MEANING
kind	caring
kindly	in a caring way
selfish	not caring about others
selfishly	in a way that does not care about others

To read a word with a suffix:

- Break the word into its parts.
- Think about the meaning of each part.
- Put the meanings together to understand the whole word.

A. Find the meaning for each underlined word.

1. Uhmma took care of her children <u>lovingly</u>.   Meaning: _____

2. Sometimes she spoke to them <u>softly</u>.   Meaning: _____

3. Other times she spoke to them <u>firmly</u>.   Meaning: _____

4. Uhmma had a hard life, but she lived it <u>beautifully</u>.   Meaning: _____

B. Read the words in the box. Add the suffix *-ly* to change the meaning. Use the right word to complete each sentence.

quiet	wild	quick	smooth

5. The martial arts contest begins. The people are excited. They cheer _____ .

6. The fighters do not wait. They _____ begin fighting.

7. The people stop making noise. They only talk _____ .

8. The contest ends _____ , without any problems.

COMPREHENSION: Cause and Effect

The cause is the reason something happens. The effect is what happens as a result.

- To find the effect, ask: "What happened?"
- To find the cause, ask: "Why did this happen?"

A. Reread the selection. Then answer the questions below.

1. What happens after Bruce uses his skills to fight?

Yip Man tells Bruce there is _____ in martial arts.

2. What happens after Bruce hits the water and sees that it does not break?

He _____ Yip Man's words.

3. What happens when Bruce calms himself?

He wins against _____ .

B. Use your answers to complete the Cause-and-Effect Chart.

Cause-and-Effect Chart

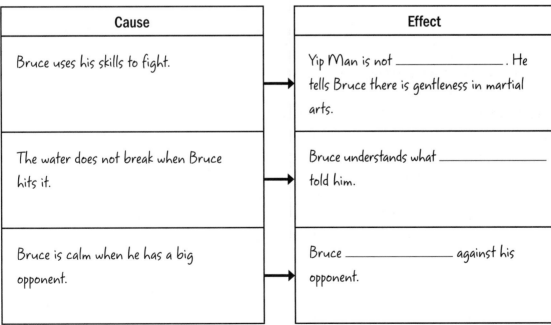

Cause	Effect
Bruce uses his skills to fight.	Yip Man is not _____ . He tells Bruce there is gentleness in martial arts.
The water does not break when Bruce hits it.	Bruce understands what _____ told him.
Bruce is calm when he has a big opponent.	Bruce _____ against his opponent.

Prepare to Read
▶ Mathematics
▶ Remember

Key Vocabulary

Circle a number to rate how well you know each word. Mark an *X* next to the correct definition to check your understanding. Then create a drawing to show the meaning of the word.

Rating Scale

1 I do not know this word.	**2** I am not sure of the word's meaning.	**3** I know this word. I can teach the word to someone else.

Key Word	Check Your Understanding	Deepen Your Understanding
❶ connect (ku-**nekt**) *verb* Rating: 1 2 3	☐ to join together ☐ to watch television	Draw two things that **connect** to each other.
❷ history (**his**-trē) *noun* Rating: 1 2 3	☐ things that happened in the past ☐ things that happen in the future	Draw an important person in **history**.
❸ joy (**joi**) *noun* Rating: 1 2 3	☐ happiness ☐ anger	Draw something that brings you **joy**.
❹ listen (**li**-sun) *verb* Rating: 1 2 3	☐ to touch ☐ to hear	Draw an instrument you **listen** to.

Sometimes **poor** people imagine being **rich**. ▶

Key Word	Check Your Understanding	Deepen Your Understanding
5 poor (**por**) *adjective* Rating: 1 2 3	☐ with a lot of money ☐ with little money	Draw something you may give to a **poor** person.
6 receive (ri-**sēv**) *verb* Rating: 1 2 3	☐ to take ☐ to give	Draw a gift you want to **receive**.
7 remember (ri-**mem**-bur) *verb* Rating: 1 2 3	☐ to grow ☐ to think of again	Draw a character you **remember** from a movie.
8 rich (**rich**) *adjective* Rating: 1 2 3	☐ with a lot of money ☐ with no money	Draw what you can buy if you are **rich**.

Before Reading Mathematics

READING STRATEGY: Ask Questions

HOW TO ASK QUESTIONS

1. Read the text. Ask yourself questions about the author's big ideas.

2. Write your questions on self-stick notes.

3. Reread or read on to find the answers.

4. If an answer is not in the text, stop and think. Think about what you know from your own life to help you find the answer.

A. Read the text. Think about the question on the self-stick note.

Look Into the Text

My great-grandmother Mina never went to school. She never learned to read. She never learned to write. And she never studied mathematics.

Why does the author say that Mina never went to school?

B. What do you know from your own life that can help you answer the question?

I know that _____

_____.

C. Now answer the question on the self-stick note.

The author tells this fact about Mina because _____

_____.

Selection Review Mathematics

 What Makes Us Wise?
Think about different kinds of wisdom.

In "Mathematics," you read about Mina's wisdom. Read the questions.
Decide if you can reread or think about what you know to find the answer.
Circle how you find the answer. Then complete the chart.

Question	Reread, or Think About What I Know?	Answer
Who was Cotita?	Reread Think	Cotita was _____ _____.
Why did the author say to herself, "Three times three is nine"?	Reread Think	She was _____ _____.
What were Mina's children like?	Reread Think	Two of them were _____, two were _____, and two were _____.
What presents did Mina receive from her visitors?	Reread Think	She received _____ _____ _____ _____.
How did Mina remember so many birthdays?	Reread Think	Mina probably _____ _____ _____ _____.

Before Reading Remember

Elements of Poetry: Repetition

HOW TO APPRECIATE REPETITION IN A POEM

1. Read the poem aloud. Listen to the sounds.

2. Listen for words that the poet repeats, or uses again and again.

3. Think about why the poet repeats a word or group of words. Ask, "How does the repetition show what is important to understand or feel?"

A. Read the lines of poetry. Which word does the poet repeat?

Look Into the Text

Remember the earth whose skin you are:
red earth, black earth, yellow earth, white earth
brown earth, we are earth.

The poet repeats the word
"_____."

B. Now think about why the poet repeats that word. What does she want you to understand or feel?

The poet wants me to understand that people are like _____. There are different _____ of earth, but they are all the same. People have different _____ of skin, but they are _____.

© NGSP & HB

Connect Across Texts

*In "Mathematics," the author **remembers** the wisdom she learned from her grandmother. Now read this poem. What does the author want you to remember?*

Remember

BY JOY HARJO

Remember the sky you were born under,
know each of the star's stories.
Remember the moon, know who she is.
Remember the sun's birth at dawn, that is the
5 strongest point of time. Remember sundown
and the giving away to night.

Key Vocabulary
remember *verb*, to think of
something again

In Other Words
sundown the time when the sun
goes down
the giving away when the sky
turns dark

Interact with the Text

1. Repetition in Poetry
Find an important word that the poet repeats in these lines. Circle it every time. Underline the four things that the poet wants the reader to remember. Then complete the sentence.

The poet repeats this
word to show that it is
important to think about

_____

_____.

2. Repetition in Poetry

Underline four things that the speaker tells the reader to remember. What is similar about these things? Complete the sentences.

These things all relate to

_____

_____

_____.

The speaker wants readers to remember _____

_____

_____

_____.

Remember your birth, how your mother struggled
to give you form and breath. You are evidence of
her life, and her mother's, and hers.

10   Remember your father. He is your life, also.
Remember the earth whose skin you are:
red earth, black earth, yellow earth, white earth
brown earth, we are earth.

In Other Words
your birth when you were born
struggled worked very hard
form and breath life
evidence alive because
your life why you are alive
whose skin you are because you are part of it

Remember the plants, trees, animal life who all have their

15 tribes, their families, their histories, too. Talk to them,
listen to them. They are alive poems.
Remember the wind. Remember her voice.
She knows the origin of this universe.

The speaker of the poem thinks that plants and animals are (similar to/ different from) people because they have

In Other Words
tribes groups
voice sounds
origin of this universe beginning of everything

4. Repetition in Poetry

What does the speaker say "you" are? Circle two things in the poem. What does the speaker say language is like?

_____

Remember you are all people and all people
20   are you.
Remember you are this universe and this
universe is you.
Remember all is in motion, is growing, is you.
Remember language comes from this.
25   Remember the dance language is, that life is.
Remember.

In Other Words
all is in motion everything is always changing
the dance how exciting and beautiful

Selection Review Remember

Reread the poem "Remember." Notice how the poet uses repetition. Think about what is important to understand and feel in the poem. Complete the chart. Use your own words or the poet's.

The poet wants readers to remember . . .	because . . .
their birth	their mothers struggled to give them _____.
the earth	people _____.
plants and animals	they are _____.
the wind	_____.
that everything is in motion	_____.
that language and life are both _____	_____.

Reflect and Assess

▶ Mathematics
▶ Remember

WRITING: Write About Literature

A. Plan your writing. Who or what do you listen to for advice? Read the examples.
Then add your own example to the chart. Use the Word Bank to help you.

Word Bank

radio	friend	aunt	counselor
mother	brother	grandmother	CDs
teacher	sister	father	grandfather
TV	uncle	coach	nature

Who or What?	Why?
I listen to the words in country music.	They make me wise because the songs tell stories about life.
I listen to my sister's advice.	My sister is a good student. Her advice makes me wise because it helps me learn how to be a good student, too.
I listen to _____ _____ for advice.	It makes me wise because _____ _____.

B. Write a journal entry. Explain how what you listen to makes you wise.
Use the example you wrote in the chart.

Paragraph Organizer

I listen to _____ for advice.

(It makes / They make) me wise because _____

_____.

I also listen to _____

because _____

_____

_____.

© NGSP & HB

Unit 2: Wisdom of the Ages   73

Integrate the Language Arts

VOCABULARY STUDY: Suffixes

A suffix is a word part added at the end of a word. A suffix changes the meaning of the word.

SUFFIX	MEANING
-able	can be done
-ly	in that way

usual + -ly = usually   **Usually** means "in a usual way."

enjoy + -able = enjoyable   **Enjoyable** means "can be enjoyed."

A. Separate the suffix from the word. Then figure out the word's meaning.

Word	Parts	Meaning
1. readable	read + -able =	
2. gladly	_____ + _____ =	
3. understandable	_____ + _____ =	
4. clearly	_____ + _____ =	
5. predictable	_____ + _____ =	

B. Circle the word that best completes the sentence.

6. Alma Flor Ada's memoir is very (breakable/readable).

7. I know how the story ends, because it is very (enjoyable/predictable).

8. Mina's children always visit her (gladly/clearly).

9. Joy Harjo's writing is (clearly/gladly) full of love for her family.

10. The poet's respect for our beautiful Earth is (understandable/readable).

Integrate the Language Arts

VOCABULARY STUDY: Compound Words

A compound word is made up of two smaller words:

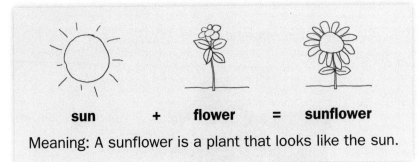

sun + **flower** = **sunflower**

Meaning: A sunflower is a plant that looks like the sun.

A. Read each compound word. Break it into its word parts.

1. notebook   ⟶   _____ + _____

2. wildflowers   ⟶   _____ + _____

3. birdbath   ⟶   _____ + _____

4. handwriting   ⟶   _____ + _____

5. childlike   ⟶   _____ + _____

6. backpack   ⟶   _____ + _____

B. Complete each sentence with one of the compound words from above.

7. Mina's son gives her some _____ in a vase.

8. A daughter places a _____ in the garden.

9. One of Mina's sons likes to write. He has beautiful _____ .

10. Mina gives him a _____ to write in.

11. When he receives the gift, his joy is _____ .

12. He puts the gift in his _____ .

Vocabulary Review

A. Study each picture. Circle the word that completes the sentence.

1.

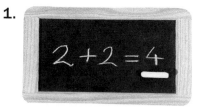

Math is easy. It is **(tough / simple)**.

2.

She needs to **(rest / touch)** after she plays soccer.

3.

When you have a lot of money you are **(rich / poor)**.

4.

My friends are not here. I feel **(difficult / lonely)**.

B. Choose words to complete the chart below.

break   **difficult**   **learn**   **rich**   **selfish**   **understand**

Word	Word Parts	New Word	Meaning of New Word
difficult	+ -ly	difficultly	like a _____ person or in a _____ way
_____	+ -able	learnable	can be learned
understand	+ -able	_____	can be understood
_____	+ -ly	selfishly	like a selfish person or in a selfish way
rich	+ -ly	_____	in a rich way
break	+ -able	breakable	can _____

Unit 2 Vocabulary

advice	explain	learn	receive	share	understand
angry	fight	listen	remember	simple	wisdom
break	harm	lonely	rest	solution	
connect	history	poor	rich	touch	
difficult	joy	problem	selfish	tough	

C. Read each sentence. Circle the word that completes the sentence correctly.

1. Our teacher helps us to (**learn / connect**) English.

2. I (**listen / harm**) to what she says.

3. She tells us about the past, or about (**history / wisdom**).

4. Her (**joy / advice**) is to study a lot.

5. After I study, I try to (**remember / break**) what I learn.

6. My friend's (**solution / problem**) is that he does not understand.

7. I do not want to be (**poor / selfish**), so I help him study.

Unit Vocabulary

Circle a number to rate how well you know each word. Circle *yes* or *no* to check your understanding. Then complete the sentences.

▲ Where do you live in the **world**?

Rating Scale

1	I do not know this word.	2	I am not sure of the word's meaning.	3	I know this word. I can teach the word to someone else.

Key Word	Check Your Understanding	Deepen Your Understanding
1 country (**kun**-trē) *noun* Rating: 1 2 3	The United States is a **country**. Every **country** has its own flag. Yes No	 Some countries I know about are _____ _____ .
2 culture (**kul**-chur) *noun* Rating: 1 2 3	Art, music, and sports are parts of a **culture**. Football is part of American **culture**. Yes No	 When you learn about another culture, you _____ _____ .
3 world (**wur**-uld) *noun* Rating: 1 2 3	The **world** is smaller than a country. Yes No	 Some ways to see the world are _____ _____ .

Vocabulary Workshop

Use Word Parts

Some English words are made up of different parts. These parts include **base words**, **prefixes**, and **suffixes**.

You can use word parts as clues to a word's meaning. Follow these steps.

- Look for a prefix or suffix. Cover it. Example: **hopeful**
- Read the base word and think about its meaning.
- Uncover the prefix or suffix and think about its meaning.
- Put the meanings of the word parts together.

SUFFIX	MEANING	EXAMPLE
-ful	full of	hope**ful**
-able	can be done	change**able**

PREFIX	MEANING	EXAMPLE
un-	not	**un**happy
re-	again	**re**write

Practice Using Word Parts

Read the passage. Circle the base word in each underlined word. Use word parts to figure out the word's definition. Complete the chart.

Earth in Danger

Some scientists say we are in danger. Some things we do are <u>unsafe</u>. They hurt the Earth. They are <u>harmful</u> for plants, animals, and people.

Word	Parts	Definition
unsafe		
harmful		

Put the Strategy to Use

Find the base word for each underlined word. Write what you think the word means.

1. Some water in the village is <u>drinkable</u>. _____

2. We feel <u>restful</u> when we look at a clean sky and beautiful trees. _____

3. We have to be <u>unselfish</u> and think about the whole Earth. _____

4. One way to keep Earth safe is to <u>reuse</u> boxes many times. _____

Prepare to Read

▶ **If the World Were a Village**
▶ **Freaky Food**

Key Vocabulary

Circle a number to rate how well you know each word. Circle *yes* or *no* to check your understanding. Then complete the sentences.

Rating Scale

| 1 | I do not know this word. | 2 | I am not sure of the word's meaning. | 3 | I know this word. I can teach the word to someone else. |

Key Word	Check Your Understanding	Deepen Your Understanding
❶ **crowded** (**krow**-dud) *adjective* Rating: 1 2 3	In a **crowded** place, you are all alone. Yes No	When a room is crowded, it is _____ _____ _____ _____ .
❷ **decide** (di-**sīd**) *verb* Rating: 1 2 3	People in a store **decide** what to buy. Yes No	Every day, I decide _____ _____ _____ _____ .
❸ **enough** (i-**nuf**) *adjective* Rating: 1 2 3	When your plate is full, you have **enough** food. Yes No	A person who eats enough food feels _____ _____ _____ _____ .
❹ **hungry** (**hung**-grē) *adjective* Rating: 1 2 3	A **hungry** person needs to get warm. Yes No	When I am hungry, I _____ _____ _____ _____ .

The **village** has 200 people. The water in this village is **safe**. ▶

Key Word	Check Your Understanding	Deepen Your Understanding
5 instead (in-**sted**) *adverb* Rating: 1 2 3	Some children work **instead** of going to school. Yes No	Instead of cars, people can ride _____ _____ _____ _____ .
6 meal (**mēl**) *noun* Rating: 1 2 3	Breakfast is the first **meal** of the day. Yes No	My favorite meal to eat is _____ _____ _____ _____ .
7 safe (**sāf**) *adjective* Rating: 1 2 3	Clean water is **safe** to drink. Yes No	One way to be safe in a car is _____ _____ _____ _____ .
8 village (**vi**-lij) *noun* Rating: 1 2 3	A **village** is bigger than a city. Yes No	If you live in a village, you might think the city is ____ _____ _____ _____ .

READING STRATEGY: Determine Importance

Reading Strategy
Determine Importance

How to DETERMINE IMPORTANCE

1. Look at the headings, pictures, and boldfaced words. Identify the topic, or what the selection is mostly about. Write it in a **Main Idea Chart**.

2. Decide what the author mostly is writing about the topic. Ask, "What is most important for me to know about the topic?"

3. Write the most important idea.

A. Read the passage and study the information in the picture.

Look Into the Text

Schooling and Literacy

A bell begins the school day. Some children in the village have no school near them. Others do. But they don't go to school. They must work instead. They help feed their families. How many people attend school?

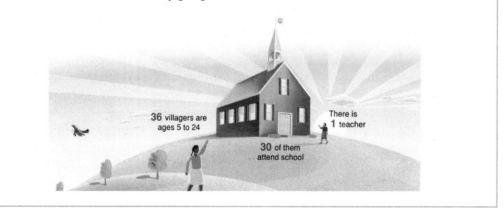

36 villagers are ages 5 to 24

There is 1 teacher

30 of them attend school

B. Now use the heading, the picture, and the text to complete the Main Idea Chart.

Main Idea Chart

Topic	Most Important Idea
	Some children do not _____ .

Selection Review If the World Were a Village

What Makes Us the Same? What Makes Us Different?
Talk about how our environments make us different.

In "If the World Were a Village," you read about how people in the world are different. Complete the Main Idea Chart with information about each section of the text. Work with a partner.

Main Idea Chart

Topic	Most Important Idea
global village	The people in the village can teach us about _____ _____ _____ _____ .
languages	There are almost _____ languages in the village. More than half the people speak _____ _____ _____ .
food	There is enough _____ _____ but many people are _____ _____ .
air and water	Most air and water in the village _____ _____ But some air and water _____ _____ .
schools	Some children in the village go _____ _____ but some _____ . Not everyone in the village can _____ _____ .

Before Reading Freaky Food

TEXT FEATURE: Headings

HOW TO USE HEADINGS

1. Read the heading to find out the topic of the section.

2. Think about what you already know about the topic. Then predict what the section is about.

3. Read the section. Check your prediction.

A. Read the heading. Use it to predict what the section is about.

The heading tells me that this section is about _____ .

Look Into the Text

EAT A WEED

Did you know you can eat some kinds of dandelions? Europeans and Americans have eaten them for centuries. The leaves make a salad. The yellow flowers can be fried. They are eaten like French fries. Make sure to wash the flowers well before you cook them.

You can cook dandelion weeds or eat them raw. ▶

B. Now read the section and say what it is about.

This section is about _____

_____ .

Freaky Food

BY NANCY SHEPHERDSON

Connect Across Texts

In "If the World Were a Village," David Smith uses numbers to show how people are different. How does the author of this magazine article show differences around the world?

Have you ever eaten ants? Kids in many countries munch on fried ants. You may say "Ewww," but it's normal for them. People eat the foods of their country. They like those foods.

In Other Words
Freaky Strange
munch on eat

1. Headings

Circle the first heading. What do you think the section is about?

The section is about _____
_____
_____.

2. Headings

What is the heading of this section? Complete the sentence.

The section is about _____
_____
_____.

YOU'RE BUGGING ME!

Insects give a lot of **energy**. **Early American pioneers** ate bugs when they didn't have other food. Ask people in Africa, Australia, Europe, Asia, and America. Many people eat insects in over half the world. They say that ants taste good.

CHICKEN FEET

Our grocery stores have a lot of food. There are still a lot of things that are hard to find there. Do you know what happens to chicken feet? Every week, the United States sends 30 million pounds of them to Asia. They are popular there.

For many people, chicken feet are a delicious treat.

In Other Words

energy power to keep your brain and body active
Early American pioneers People who traveled across the United States in the late 1700s and throughout the 1800s

EAT A WEED

Did you know you can eat some kinds of dandelions? Europeans and Americans have eaten them for **centuries**. The leaves make a salad. The yellow flowers can be fried. They are eaten like French fries. Make sure to wash the flowers well before you cook them. **Seaweed is** also very popular. It is in many of the foods we eat every day. Your hamburger might have some seaweed. Your ice cream might, too. Bet you can't taste it.

WHAT'S ON THE MENU?

Different foods are eaten around the world. That is no surprise. The people of the world are very different, too. We have different cultures. We may believe different things. Our countries grow different foods. Some people are lucky. They have a lot of food. Others are not as lucky. They eat what they can find.

All of these things are important. They help us **decide** which foods to eat. They give us different **tastes**.

You can cook dandelion weeds or eat them raw.

Key Vocabulary
decide *verb*, to make a choice

In Other Words
Weed Wild plant
centuries hundreds of years
Seaweed is Plants that grow in the sea are
tastes ideas about what we like

3. Headings
Read the heading. Predict what you think this section is about.

I predict that this section is about _____

_____

_____.

Read on to find out what the section is about.

4. Headings
Read the heading. Then read the section and complete the sentence.

People in different countries _____

_____

_____.

Try a little test. At lunch today, look around. What "freaky foods" do you see? Before you say "Ewww," look at your own lunch. What would other people say? Your favorite **meal** may be a "freaky food" to **your neighbor**. That's OK. Our foods can be different and special—just like all the people in the world. ❖

Key Vocabulary
meal *noun*, all the food you eat at one time

In Other Words
Try a little test. Do something new.
your neighbor the person next to you

Selection Review Freaky Food

Complete the chart. Read each heading. Then write what the section is about.

Heading	Topic
You're Bugging Me!	Many people eat _____.
Chicken Feet	Many people like _____.
Eat a Weed	Some popular foods are _____ _____.
What's on the Menu?	People eat different foods because _____ _____.

Reflect and Assess

WRITING: Write About Literature

A. Read the opinion statement.

> **Opinion Statement:** People are mainly the same everywhere.

Tell if you agree or disagree with the statement. Then complete the sentence to support your opinion. Use examples from the selections.

1. State Your Opinion	2. Support Your Opinion
I agree/disagree that people are mainly the same everywhere.	I think this because _____ _____ .

B. Finish this paragraph to express your opinion. Say whether you think people are mainly the same or different throughout the world. Use your notes.

Paragraph Organizer

In my opinion, people are mainly _____ throughout the world. I believe

this because _____ . In "If the World Were a

Village," the author explains that _____

_____ . This example shows that

_____ . Another example of how people are

(the same/different) comes from the article _____ . In this article, the

author explains that _____

_____ . These examples clearly show how people are basically

(the same/different) everywhere.

Integrate the Language Arts

VOCABULARY STUDY: Review Suffixes

A suffix is a word part added to the end of a base word. It changes the meaning of the word.

SUFFIX	MEANING	EXAMPLE
-er	person who does this action	read + **-er** = reader (person who reads) He is a good **reader** because he reads a lot.
-y	having the quality of; like	dirt + **-y** = dirty (with dirt; having dirt) His boots got **dirty** when he stepped in the mud.

A. Add a word to complete each sentence. Use the correct suffix at the end of the word.

   1. A person who teaches is a _____ .

   2. Someone who sings is a _____ .

   3. A place with many rocks is _____ .

   4. When you have thirst, you are _____ .

B. Read each sentence. Write the meaning of the underlined word.

   5. Ray is the best <u>catcher</u> on our baseball team.

   _____

   6. Gita takes her camera everywhere. She is a <u>photographer</u>.

   _____

   7. My parents get angry about my <u>messy</u> room.

   _____

   8. Mariah visits many countries. She is a <u>traveler</u>.

   _____

RESEARCH/SPEAKING: Use a Bar Graph

Graphs give information with numbers and words. Look at the graph below.

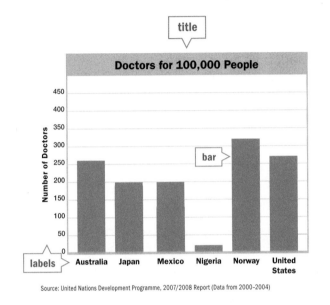

Source: United Nations Development Programme, 2007/2008 Report (Data from 2000-2004)

A. Read the title and the labels.

1. What is the title of the graph? _____

2. What is the label for the numbers at the left side? _____

3. What do these numbers show? _____

4. What are some labels from the bottom of the graph? _____

5. What do these labels tell? _____

B. Work with a partner. Point to a country. Move your finger up the bar. Then read across to find the number of doctors.

1. How many doctors does Australia have for every 100,000 people? _____

2. How many doctors does Japan have for every 100,000 people? _____

Prepare to Read

▶ **Behind the Veil**
▶ **The Simple Sport**

Key Vocabulary

Circle a number to rate how well you know each word. Mark an *X* next to the correct definition to check your understanding. Then create a drawing to show the meaning of each word.

Rating Scale

1 I do not know this word.	**2** I am not sure of the word's meaning.	**3** I know this word. I can teach the word to someone else.

Key Word	Check Your Understanding	Deepen Your Understanding
❶ **belief** (bu-**lēf**) *noun* **Rating: 1 2 3**	☐ an idea that you think is true ☐ a subject that you study	Draw a picture of a **belief** a small child may have.
❷ **experience** (ik-**spear**-ē-uns) *noun* **Rating: 1 2 3**	☐ something that you did or saw ☐ something that you found	Draw an **experience** you can have in the summer.
❸ **forget** (fur-**get**) *verb* **Rating: 1 2 3**	☐ to not be able to see something ☐ to not be able to think of something	Draw something you use when you **forget** a phone number.
❹ **popular** (**pah**-pyu-lur) *adjective* **Rating: 1 2 3**	☐ something that nobody likes ☐ something that many people like	Draw a **popular** food.

Baseball is a **popular sport**. ▶

Key Word	Check Your Understanding	Deepen Your Understanding
⑤ religion (ri-**li**-jun) *noun* Rating: 1 2 3	☐ the study of history ☐ a set of strong ideas about a god or gods	Draw a place where people practice their **religion**.
⑥ sport (**sport**) *noun* Rating: 1 2 3	☐ a game, such as baseball or basketball ☐ a class, such as math or science	Draw something you can use to play a **sport**.
⑦ truth (**trüth**) *noun* Rating: 1 2 3	☐ something that is wrong ☐ something that is a fact	Draw someone who asks you to tell the **truth**.
⑧ uncomfortable (un-**kumf**-tur-bul) *adjective* Rating: 1 2 3	☐ feeling easy ☐ not feeling easy	Draw the face of someone who feels **uncomfortable**.

Before Reading Behind the Veil

READING STRATEGY: Determine Importance

> **Reading Strategy**
> **Determine Importance**

HOW TO SUMMARIZE A PARAGRAPH

1. Identify the topic. Ask, "What is the paragraph mostly about?"

2. As you read, take notes about the important details and ideas. Use a **Summary Planner**.

3. Stop and ask, "What does the author want me to know in this part of the selection?" Write a sentence or two to retell the ideas.

A. Read the text.

> **Look Into the Text**
>
> We had all tried to make her feel welcome many times throughout the week. Sometimes she seemed depressed. We tried to make her laugh. Other times she seemed lonely. We tried to start conversations with her. She rarely lifted her head to look at us. When she did, we saw her sad eyes. They seemed full of emotion. It was waiting to pour out.

B. Complete the Summary Planner.

Summary Planner

Title: _____
Topic: _____
Important Details and Ideas: • Students tried to _____   • _____   • _____
Sum Up the Ideas: The girl seemed _____   _____

Selection Review Behind the Veil

EQ **What Makes Us the Same? What Makes Us Different?**
Think about how the experiences we share make us the same.

In "Behind the Veil," you read about how people who seem different may be the same in many ways.

Complete the Summary Planner. Underline the important ideas and details in each paragraph. Then sum up the ideas.

Summary Planner

Title: Behind the Veil	
Important Details and Ideas	**Sum Up the Ideas**
When everyone finished speaking, Nadia slowly rose from the corner. She walked to the middle of the room. "This has been a memorable week," she said. "But it has also been one of my most uncomfortable."	Nadia tells the other students that the week was _____ _____ .
"All of you have been wonderful to me," she said. "But I realize that some of you are afraid of me and my beliefs. I understand. You only know the Islam that you hear about in the media. You don't know the truth of our religion."	Nadia says the other students are _____ _____ She says they don't know a lot about _____ _____ .
What she said was true. We knew about the beliefs of Islamic terrorists. But we knew nothing about the beliefs of nonviolent Muslims. I didn't know anything about her religion.	The writer agrees with Nadia. He says the other students know nothing about _____ _____ _____ .
"The truth is that I am just like all of you. I like the same music. I like the same television shows." A single tear slid down her cheek. "When you laugh at something, so do I. And when you cry, I do, too."	Nadia tells the other students that she is ____ _____ _____ .
Nadia's words were simple. They meant so much to me. Her clothing and religion did not define her. She was a teenager growing up in America—just like me.	The writer now understands that he and Nadia _____ _____

TEXT FEATURE: Globes

HOW TO LOCATE A COUNTRY ON A GLOBE

1. Read the name of the country in the text.

2. Look for the country on the globe.

3. Read the labels to see what continent the country is part of. The names of continents are in capital letters.

4. Think about where the country is located. Use this information to help you understand the text.

Read the text and find the country on the globe. Think about where the country is located. Then complete the sentences.

Look Into the Text

▶ZAMBIA

Zambia's national soccer team formed in 1929. The team is practicing for the 2010 World Cup in South Africa.

AFRICA

Zambia

The name of the country shown is

_____.

It is on the continent of

_____.

Zambia is _____

the equator.

The Simple Sport

by Sara Chiu

Connect Across Texts

In "Behind the Veil," the author learns he has many things in common with someone from another culture. In this photo essay, learn how many countries share a love of soccer.

Call it soccer, football, or *fútbol*. It is one **sport** with many names. In the United States, we call it soccer. It's the most **popular** sport in the world.

Soccer is called "the simple sport." You can see why. It's a game anyone can play. Players are young and old. They are male and female. They are rich and poor. Soccer is a sport everyone can enjoy.

Soccer is a very old sport. The Chinese played games like soccer thousands of years ago. It was also played in Rome, Egypt, Europe, and Central America. These games changed over time. One thing has never changed. Soccer is still **exciting**.

Is soccer still popular today? Ask billions of soccer fans. They sit in crowded **stadiums**. They watch from their TVs. They **cheer** for their favorite **teams**. Ask millions of soccer players. They play in schoolyards. They play on fields. They play in stadiums. Soccer is the sport they love.

Let's see how soccer is played around the world.

Key Vocabulary
sport *noun*, game
popular *adjective*, liked by many people

In Other Words
fútbol soccer (in Spanish)
exciting a lot of fun
stadiums large, open places for playing and watching sports
cheer shout with happiness
teams groups of players

1. Locate a Country on a Globe

Which country is this section about?

This section is about

_____

_____ .

What continent is it on?

It is on the continent of

_____

_____ .

2. Locate a Country on a Globe

Circle the countries that are mentioned here. What continent are they on?

They are on the continent of

_____

_____ .

▶ ENGLAND

England has one of the oldest national soccer teams. It started in 1872. Soccer is England's most popular sport. It's also **a big business**. England's soccer team uses this flag.

▶ SOUTH KOREA

Many people play soccer in South Korea. It had one of the first **professional teams** in East Asia. South Korea and Japan **hosted** the World Cup in 2002.

In Other Words

a big business an activity that makes money
professional teams groups of people who were paid to play
hosted organized

Cultural Background

The World Cup is a tournament of soccer games to decide the best soccer team in the world. The World Cup takes place every four years, and a different country hosts the games each time.

▶ ZAMBIA

Zambia's national soccer team **formed** in 1929. The team is practicing for the 2010 World Cup in South Africa.

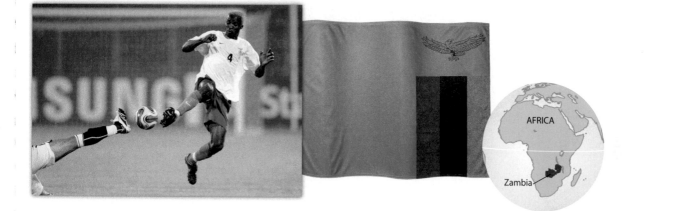

▶ BRAZIL

Soccer is important in the culture of Brazil. Its team has been in every World Cup final. Brazil won the World Cup for the first time in 1958. Brazil has won four more times since then.

In Other Words
formed started

▶ UNITED STATES

Soccer is more popular every year in the U.S. It is played across the country. You just need a ball and some friends. Come play "the simple sport." ❖

<table>
</table>

Interact with the Text

4. Locate a Country on a Globe

Circle the country that this section is about.

What continent is it on?

It is on the continent of

_____

_____ .

Selection Review The Simple Sport

This photo essay mentions places around the world that share a love for soccer. Complete the chart below. Match the countries to their continents.

Countries	Continent	Above or Below Equator
_____	North America	_____
Egypt, _____	Africa	_____
England	_____	_____
China, _____, and _____	Asia	_____
_____	South America	_____

Reflect and Assess

WRITING: Write About Literature

A. Plan your writing. Reread "Behind the Veil" and "The Simple Sport." Think about what the Presidential Classroom and a sports team are about. Then complete the chart.

Activity	Why People Like It	Who Can Join
Presidential Classroom	You meet other students from all over the country.	Boys and girls can join.
Soccer		

B. Write an invitation. Use the student model as a guide.

Student Model

> Join the Presidential Classroom.
> Everyone in this group likes to meet students from all over the world.
> You can be a boy or girl.
> Join now!

Organizer

Join the _____.

Everyone in this group likes _____.

You can be _____ or _____. Join now!

VOCABULARY STUDY: Review Prefixes

A prefix is a word part added to the beginning of a base word. It changes the meaning of the word.

PREFIX	MEANING	EXAMPLE
un-	not	**un-** + safe = unsafe It is **unsafe** to drive without a seatbelt.
re-	again	**re-** + connect = reconnect When summer is over, I **reconnect** with my friends at school.

When you come to a word you don't know:

- Look for a prefix.
- Put the meaning of the prefix together with the meaning of the base word.
- Use the two meanings to figure out the meaning of the word.

A. Add a prefix to the beginning of each base word to match the definition.

1. not selfish: _____ selfish

2. not happy: _____ happy

3. view again: _____ view

4. place again: _____ place

5. learn again: _____ learn

6. write again: _____ write

7. not true: _____ true

8. not afraid: _____ afraid

B. Circle the word that completes each sentence. Use a dictionary for help.

9. We were (**untrue / unhappy**) when our soccer team lost the game.

10. The coach likes to (**review / replace**) the game with us when it is over.

11. At soccer practice, we (**relearn / rewrite**) our skills.

12. We play tough teams, but we are (**unhappy / unafraid**) of them.

COMPREHENSION: Classify and Compare

To classify means to put things that are alike into groups, or categories. This Category Diagram shows one way to classify the facts in "The Simple Sport."

Category Diagram

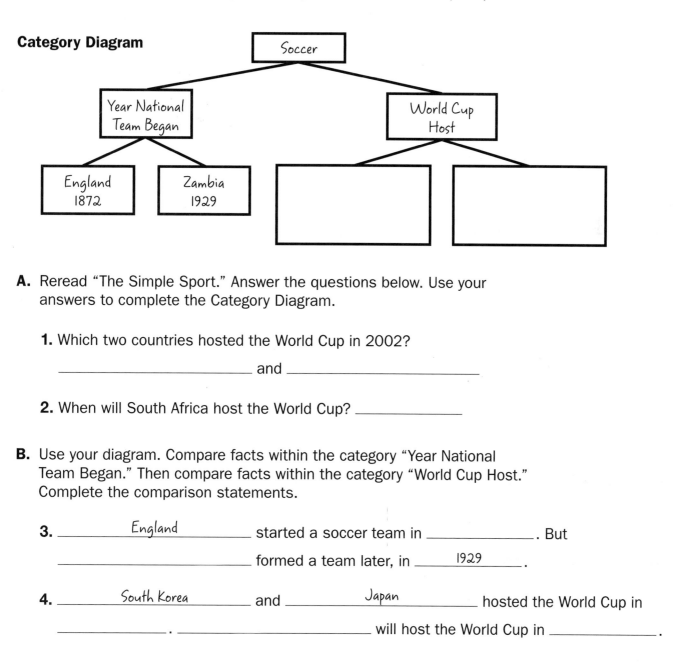

A. Reread "The Simple Sport." Answer the questions below. Use your answers to complete the Category Diagram.

1. Which two countries hosted the World Cup in 2002?

_____ and _____

2. When will South Africa host the World Cup? _____

B. Use your diagram. Compare facts within the category "Year National Team Began." Then compare facts within the category "World Cup Host." Complete the comparison statements.

3. _____England_____ started a soccer team in _____. But

_____ formed a team later, in _____1929_____ .

4. _____South Korea_____ and _____Japan_____ hosted the World Cup in

_____ . _____ will host the World Cup in _____ .

Prepare to Read

▶ **Alphabet City Ballet**
▶ **You Can Get It If You Really Want**

Key Vocabulary

Circle a number to rate how well you know each word. Circle the word that completes the sentence to check your understanding. Then write a definition.

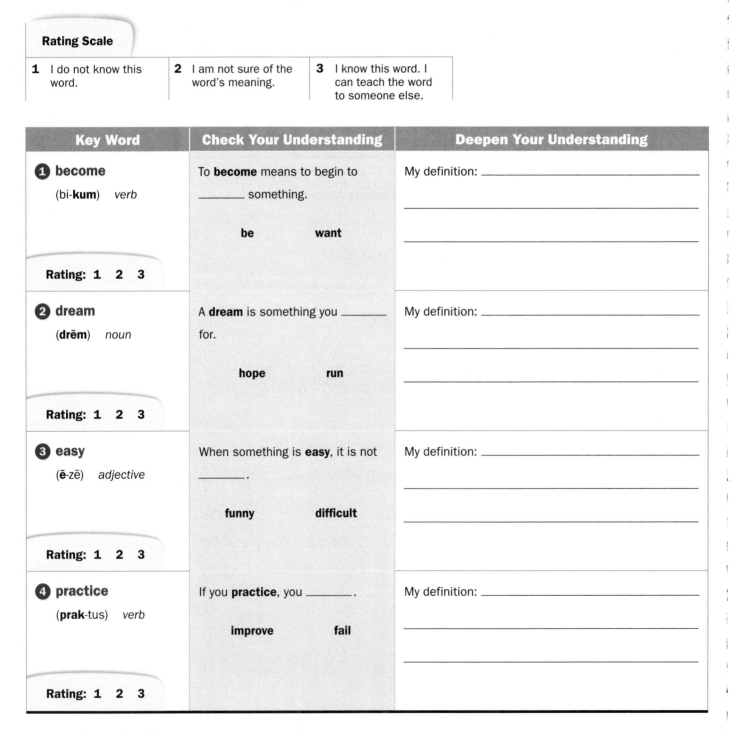

Rating Scale

| **1** I do not know this word. | **2** I am not sure of the word's meaning. | **3** I know this word. I can teach the word to someone else. |

Key Word	Check Your Understanding	Deepen Your Understanding
1 become (bi-**kum**) *verb* Rating: 1 2 3	To **become** means to begin to _____ something. be want	My definition: _____ _____ _____
2 dream (**drēm**) *noun* Rating: 1 2 3	A **dream** is something you _____ for. hope run	My definition: _____ _____ _____
3 easy (**ē**-zē) *adjective* Rating: 1 2 3	When something is **easy**, it is not _____. funny difficult	My definition: _____ _____ _____
4 practice (**prak**-tus) *verb* Rating: 1 2 3	If you **practice**, you _____. improve fail	My definition: _____ _____ _____

I have **respect** for people who **succeed.** ▶

Key Word	Check Your Understanding	Deepen Your Understanding
5 **respect** (ri-**spekt**) *noun* Rating: 1 2 3	When you show **respect**, you show that you _____ someone or something. **value** **dislike**	My definition: _____ _____ _____
6 **succeed** (suk-**sēd**) *verb* Rating: 1 2 3	To **succeed** is to _____ a goal. **miss** **reach**	My definition: _____ _____ _____
7 **try** (**trī**) *verb* Rating: 1 2 3	To **try** means to make an _____. **idea** **effort**	My definition: _____ _____ _____
8 **victory** (**vik**-tu-rē) *noun* Rating: 1 2 3	When you achieve a **victory**, you _____. **lose** **win**	My definition: _____ _____ _____

Before Reading Alphabet City Ballet

READING STRATEGY: Determine Importance

HOW TO DETERMINE WHAT'S IMPORTANT TO YOU

1. Look for details. Think about what the characters say. Pay attention to details that remind you of your own life. Ask, "Is my life similar to this? Is it different?"

2. Note these details. Make a **T Chart**. In the first column, write important words and phrases from the text.

3. In the second column, write about why the text is meaningful to you.

4. Reread your chart. Which details are the most important to you?

A. Read the text and look for details.

> **Look Into the Text**
>
> She bit her lip. "I want to wear your sweatband Wednesday. I wanted to try it on. For ballet."
> "You don't raise no sweat in 'ballet.'" He said "ballet" so that it sounded like "sweat."

B. Now complete the T Chart.

T Chart

What I Read	Why It Is Important to Me
He said "ballet" so _____	I think Luis is _____
_____	_____
_____	_____
_____	_____
_____	_____
_____ "	_____ .

Selection Review Alphabet City Ballet

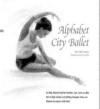

 What Makes Us the Same? What Makes Us Different?
Find out how our hopes and dreams make us different.

In "Alphabet City Ballet," you found out how one person's dreams can be very different from another's.

Reread the story. Then complete the chart. Tell why the text is important to you.

T Chart

What I Read	Why It Is Important to Me
"I'm doing something good." Her voice broke. She was on the edge of tears. (page 216)	Marisol feels _____ _____. I feel this way when _____ _____ _____
"I didn't know you took it that seriously," he said. "I do." She turned from him. "It's my dream." (page 216)	I understand how _____ feels about ballet because I _____ _____.
"A dream isn't about things," Marisol said. "A dream is who you want to be." (page 217)	My dream is to be _____ _____.
He laughed and sat up. Marisol sat up, too. They were on the floor together. Just like when they were kids, she thought. (page 218)	Marisol feels _____ because _____ _____. I sometimes feel this way when ___ _____ _____
Finally, finally, he was showing respect. It was good to feel tight with him again. (page 220)	Marisol feels _____ _____. Respect is important in a family because _____ _____ _____

Before Reading You Can Get It If You Really Want

Elements of Poetry: Rhythm, Rhyme, and Repetition

HOW TO READ SONG LYRICS

1. Read the text aloud.

2. Notice patterns. Look for words that rhyme. Look for lines that repeat.

3. Listen for a beat, or rhythm.

4. Ask, "How does the rhythm, rhyme, or repetition add to the song? How do the lyrics make me feel?" Write your ideas on self-stick notes.

A. Read the lyrics. Think about rhythm, rhyme, and repetition. Then complete the self-stick notes.

Look Into the Text

10 *You can get it if you really want*

You can get it if you really want

You can get it if you really want

But you must try, try and try, try and try

You'll succeed at last

Lines 10, _____,
and _____
repeat. The repetition
adds to the song

because _____
_____
_____.

B. Write how the lyrics make you feel.

The song lyrics make me feel _____
_____.

Connect Across Texts

In "Alphabet City Ballet," Marisol works hard to make her **dream** come true. What do these song lyrics say about dreams?

YOU CAN GET IT / IF YOU REALLY WANT

by Jimmy Cliff

Illustrations by CJ Zea

Interact with the Text

1. Song Lyrics

Read lines 6–9. Circle the words that rhyme. What do the lyrics tell you about life?

The lyrics say that

You can get it if you really want

You can get it if you really want

You can get it if you really want

But you must try, try and try, try and try

5 You'll succeed at last

Persecution you must bear

Win or lose you got to get your share

Got your mind set on a dream

You can get it though hard it may seem now

Key Vocabulary
dream *noun*, something you hope for
succeed *verb*, to reach a goal

In Other Words
Persecution you must bear You must deal with people who treat you badly
your share the part that you should have
set on always thinking about

10   *You can get it if you really want*

You can get it if you really want

You can get it if you really want

But you must try, try and try, try and try

You'll succeed at last

15   Rome was not built in a day

Opposition will come your way

But the harder the battle you see

It's the sweeter the victory

Key Vocabulary
victory *noun*, a win

In Other Words
Rome was not built in a day It may not happen quickly
Opposition Problems
battle work
sweeter better

You can get it if you really want

20 *You can get it if you really want*

You can get it if you really want

But you must try, try and try, try and try

You'll succeed at last

You can get it if you really want

25 *You can get it if you really want*

You can get it if you really want

But you must try, try and try, try and try

You'll succeed at last ❖

Interact with the Text

3. Song Lyrics

Read lines 19–28. Underline an example of repetition. How do these lines make you feel?

The lines make me feel

Selection Review You Can Get It If You Really Want

Rhyme, rhythm, and repetition are three ways to make language musical. Complete the chart. Say whether the lines add rhyme, rhythm, and/or repetition to the song. Then write how the lines make you feel.

Lines	Rhyme, Rhythm, Repetition	Feelings
Persecution you must bear Win or lose you got to get your share	☐ Rhyme ☐ Rhythm ☐ Repetition	The lines make me understand that _____ _____ .

You can get it if you really
    want
You can get it if you really
    want
	☐ Rhyme
	☐ Rhythm
	☐ Repetition
		When I read the lines I feel
		_____
		_____ .

But the harder the battle you see It's the sweeter the victory	☐ Rhyme ☐ Rhythm ☐ Repetition	The lines make me feel _____ .
But you must try, try and try, try and try You'll succeed at last	☐ Rhyme ☐ Rhythm ☐ Repetition	I like/don't like these words because _____ _____ .

Reflect and Assess

Alphabet City Ballet
You Can Get It If You Really Want

WRITING: Write About Literature

A. Plan your writing. Reread the selections to find out what each tells you about reaching a dream. Then fill in the chart about your dream.

My Dream	What the Text Tells Me	How to Reach My Dream
My dream is to become _____ _____.	The story/song tells me _____ _____ _____.	To reach my dream, I will _____ _____ _____.

B. Write a journal entry about reaching a dream. Use the student model as a guide.

Student Model

> My dream is to become a doctor because I want to help people. The story "Alphabet City Ballet" tells me I must be serious about reaching my dream. To reach my dream, I will be strong and I will work hard.

Paragraph Organizer

My dream is _____ because I want to

_____ . The story/lyrics to

_____

tells/tell me _____ .

I will _____

_____ .

© NGSP & HB

Unit 3: Global Village   113

Integrate the Language Arts

VOCABULARY STUDY: Review Prefixes, Suffixes, and Compound Words

To read a long word, break it into parts.

un- + fair = unfair   **quiet + -ly = quietly**   **every + thing = everything**

Remember these prefixes and suffixes:

PREFIX	MEANING	EXAMPLE
un-	not	unpopular
re-	again	repaint

PREFIX	MEANING	EXAMPLE
-able	can be done	enjoyable
-er	one who	teacher
-ly	in a certain way	softly

A. Break each underlined word into word parts. Then write the word's meaning.

1. Marisol knows her dream is <u>reachable</u>.

_____ + _____ = _____

2. It is <u>unfair</u> that Luis thinks Marisol's dream is not important.

_____ + _____ = _____

3. He thinks it's harder to be a soccer <u>player</u>.

_____ + _____ = _____

4. But Marisol gets Luis to think <u>differently</u>.

_____ + _____ = _____

B. Add a base word to complete each compound word. Use a dictionary to check your answers.

5. A person who writes songs is a ____song____ writer.

6. Work you do at home is called home _____ .

7. A dream you have during the day is called a day _____ .

8. You brush your hair with a _____ brush.

LITERARY ANALYSIS: Literary Element: Setting

The setting of a story is when and where it takes place. You can use clues in the story to figure out the setting.

To find a setting, follow these steps.

- Read the text.
- Look for clues that show a year, a season, or a time of day.
- Look for clues that show a location.
- Record information in your Setting Chart.

A. Review the paragraph from "Growing Together." Circle clues that help you figure out the setting.

> Some days I still miss Cuba. I miss warm breezes. I miss
>
> mango trees. I live in Georgia now. The days are cold.
>
> We only have one tree. It is a magnolia. It only grows flowers.

1. The season is _____.

I know this because of the clue, _____.

2. The character lives in _____.

I know this because of the clue, _____.

B. Use your answers from Part A to fill in the Setting Chart.

Setting Chart

Clue	Time	Place
I live in Georgia now.		
The days are cold.		

Vocabulary Review

A. Study each picture. Circle the word that completes each sentence.

1. This bus is (**crowded / instead**) with too many people.

3. For most people, dinner is the last (**meal / religion**) of the day.

2. The men bow to show each other (**belief / respect**).

4. We had a great (**village / experience**) last week.

B. Choose words to complete the webs below.

| become | decide | hungry | practice | succeed |
| crowded | forget | popular | safe | uncomfortable |

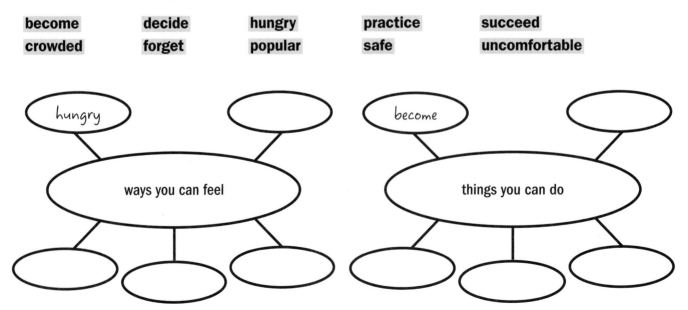

hungry

ways you can feel

become

things you can do

become	decide	forget	practice	succeed	village
belief	dream	hungry	religion	truth	world
country	easy	instead	respect	try	
culture	enough	meal	safe	uncomfortable	
crowded	experience	popular	sport	victory	

C. Read each sentence. Circle the word that completes each sentence correctly.

1. Don't (**try / forget**) an important day.

2. If you work hard, you will (**decide / succeed**) and do well.

3. I love the music that belongs to my country's (**culture / victory**).

4. My aunt enjoys the (**sport / country**) of basketball.

5. The (**world / dream**) is a large place.

6. We felt (**uncomfortable / popular**) because of the hot sun.

7. My favorite (**truth / meal**) is tacos and beans.

8. If you eat (**easy / enough**) food, you are full.

Unit Vocabulary

Circle a number to rate how well you know each word. Circle *yes* or *no* to check your understanding. Then complete the sentences.

▲ We need food to **survive**. Having no food can be an **emergency**.

Rating Scale

1 I do not know this word.	**2** I am not sure of the word's meaning.	**3** I know this word. I can teach the word to someone else.

Key Word	Check Your Understanding	Deepen Your Understanding
❶ **survive** (sur-**vīv**) *verb* **Rating: 1 2 3**	People must have water to **survive**. **Yes** **No**	 To **survive**, people must have _____ _____ _____ .
❷ **emergency** (i-**mur**-junt-sē) *noun* **Rating: 1 2 3**	When you spill water, it is usually an **emergency**. **Yes** **No**	 In an **emergency**, you must _____ _____ _____ .
❸ **instinct** (**in**-stingkt) *noun* **Rating: 1 2 3**	We have an **instinct** to open our eyes when we look at the sun. **Yes** **No**	 People have an **instinct** to run away from _____ _____ _____ .

Vocabulary Workshop

Use a Dictionary

When you read, you may see a word that you do not know. Use the dictionary to learn more about the word. Look at these parts of a dictionary page.

- **Entries** are in alphabetical order in a dictionary.
- **Guide words** show the first and last entries on a page.
- The **definition** tells what the word means.
- The **part of speech** tells how to use the word.

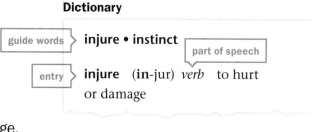

Dictionary

guide words — **injure • instinct**

part of speech

entry — **injure** (**in**-jur) *verb* to hurt or damage

instinct (**in**-stingkt) *noun* an inner ability to respond to a certain kind of situation

Practice Using a Dictionary

Read the paragraph to the right. Use the dictionary page above to answer the questions.

1. Is *injure* the first or last entry on the page?

_____

2. What part of speech is *injure*? _____

3. What is the definition of *injure*? _____

4. Rewrite the second sentence of the paragraph in your own words. _____

_____

> Animals have an <u>instinct</u> to keep away from fire. They know fire can <u>injure</u> them. Humans do not have this <u>instinct</u>. Luckily, children learn fast!

Put the Strategy to Use

Work with a partner. Read aloud the paragraph above. Use the dictionary page above the paragraph to answer the questions.

5. Is *instinct* the first or last entry on the page? _____

6. What is the definition of *instinct*? _____

7. What part of speech is *instinct*? _____

8. Explain the first and third sentences of the paragraph in your own words. _____

_____

▶ **Two Were Left**
▶ **Tornado Survivor Called "the Luckiest Man on Earth"**

Prepare to Read

Key Vocabulary

Circle a number to rate how well you know each word. Circle *yes* or *no* to check your understanding. Then create a drawing to show the meaning of the word.

Rating Scale

1 I do not know this word.	2 I am not sure of the word's meaning.	3 I know this word. I can teach the word to someone else.

Key Word	Check Your Understanding	Deepen Your Understanding
1 damage (**da**-mij) *noun* Rating: 1 2 3	A big storm can cause much **damage** to trees. Yes No	Draw a house with **damage** from a fire.
2 defenseless (di-**fens**-lus) *adjective* Rating: 1 2 3	Soldiers are **defenseless** people. Yes No	Draw a **defenseless** animal and an animal that may harm it.
3 die (**dī**) *verb* Rating: 1 2 3	All plants and animals **die**. Yes No	Draw flowers that are going to **die**.
4 fear (**fear**) *noun* Rating: 1 2 3	If you feel **fear**, you are very happy. Yes No	Draw an animal that you **fear**.

The **injured** player felt **weak**. ▶

Key Word	Check Your Understanding	Deepen Your Understanding
5 injured (**in**-jurd) *adjective* Rating: 1 2 3	We took care of the **injured** bird, and it got better. Yes No	Draw an **injured** person.
6 powerful (**pow**-ur-ful) *adjective* Rating: 1 2 3	A **powerful** wind blew in, and no one felt it. Yes No	Draw a **powerful** animal.
7 recover (ri-**ku**-vur) *verb* Rating: 1 2 3	Medicine can help a sick person **recover**. Yes No	Draw a place where people **recover** from an injury or sickness.
8 weak (wēk) *adjective* Rating: 1 2 3	A **weak** person has great power and strength. Yes No	Draw a person who looks **weak**.

READING STRATEGY: Plan and Monitor

HOW TO PREVIEW AND PREDICT

1. Read the title. Look at the pictures.

2. Begin to read. Stop after every few paragraphs to make a prediction, or decide what will happen next. Record your idea in a **Prediction Chart**.

3. Read on to find out what happens. Make a note in your chart. Decide if your prediction was confirmed, or came true.

4. Keep reading. Follow these steps to make and confirm more predictions.

A. Look at the picture and read the first part of the text.

Look Into the Text

A weapon, like a knife, was needed.
   Removing his mittens, he unstrapped the brace from his leg.

    * * * * * * * * *

   He worked all night. At dawn, his task was complete.
   Noni pulled the finished knife from the ice.

B. Make a prediction about the first part of the text. Then read on to confirm it.

Prediction Chart

What the Pictures and Text Tell Me	My Prediction	What Happens
It looks like Noni is _____ _____ . The text says _____ .	Noni will _____ _____ _____ .	_____ _____ _____

Selection Review Two Were Left

EQ ## What Does It Take to Survive?
Think about how luck helps survivors.

A. In "Two Were Left," you read about a boy and a dog who needed luck to survive. Use the Prediction Chart to write three predictions you made about the story. Then write whether your prediction came true.

Prediction Chart

What the Pictures and Text Tell Me	My Prediction	What Happens
The dog looks _____. Noni feels _____.	Noni will not be able to _____ _____ _____.	_____ _____ _____
The dog looks _____. Noni gets ready for _____ _____.	_____ _____ _____	_____ _____ _____
Noni and Nimuk look _____. An airplane _____.	_____ _____ _____	_____ _____ _____

B. Use your chart to answer the questions. Circle *yes* or *no*. Then explain your prediction.

1. Did you predict that Noni would make a knife? Yes/No, because _____

_____.

2. Did you predict that Noni would kill Nimuk? Yes/No, because _____

_____.

3. Did you predict that Noni and Nimuk would be saved? Yes/No, because _____

_____.

TEXT FEATURE: Photos and Captions

HOW TO USE PHOTOS AND CAPTIONS

1. Look at the photo.

2. Read the caption. Use the caption to understand what the photo shows.

3. Read the text. Connect the information from the photo and caption to the text.

4. Use all of the information to improve your understanding of the text.

A. Sometimes there is a map instead of a photo. You can use the same rules. Look at this map. Read the caption. Then complete the sentence in the thought bubble.

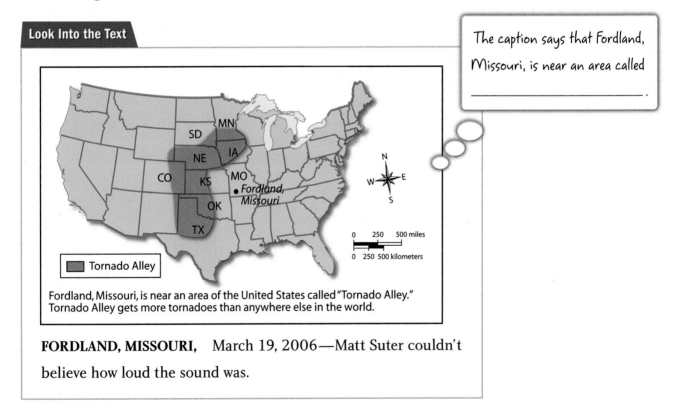

Look Into the Text

The caption says that Fordland, Missouri, is near an area called _____.

Fordland, Missouri, is near an area of the United States called "Tornado Alley." Tornado Alley gets more tornadoes than anywhere else in the world.

Tornado Alley

FORDLAND, MISSOURI, March 19, 2006—Matt Suter couldn't believe how loud the sound was.

B. Now read the text from the article. Connect the map to the text. Complete the sentence.

The text begins with the words "FORDLAND, MISSOURI." The map helps me understand the text because _____ _____ .

NEWSPAPER ARTICLE

Connect Across Texts

In "Two Were Left," Noni fights to survive. This newspaper article is about another young man who survives. Compare their stories. What did it take for them to survive?

Tornado Survivor

Called "the luckiest man on earth"

Adaptation of an article by Wes Johnson
News-Leader

AMAZING JOURNEY

FORDLAND, MISSOURI, March 19, 2006—Matt Suter couldn't believe how loud the sound was. It came from outside the trailer home's walls.

The Fordland High School senior stood on a sofa. He struggled to close a window. Outside, rain and wind hit the **trailer**.

"It got louder and louder. It sounded like ten military jets were coming at us," Suter said.

"Suddenly there was lots of **pressure**. The doors blew out. I looked at my grandma. The walls were moving. The roof was moving. The floor was moving just like Jell-O. I could feel the whole trailer **tipping over**."

In Other Words
trailer small building
pressure pushing
tipping over falling on its side

Interact with the Text

1. Preview and Predict
Read the title. Then look at the pictures in the article. What do you think this article is about?

I think this is about

_____

_____

_____

_____

2. Photos and Captions

Captions help connect photos to the text. What would be a good caption for this photo? Write it below the photo.

3. Preview and Predict

Look at the photo on this page. What do you think will happen to Matt Suter?

I think that _____

_____

_____

_____ .

A heavy lamp hit Suter in the head. He **lost consciousness**. In an instant, the tornado sucked Suter through the **collapsing** trailer walls.

Blown by **150-mile-per-hour** winds, the unconscious teen was then pulled up into the **raging blackness**.

Suter eventually landed in a field. He was **dazed** and his head was **injured**. But otherwise, he was not hurt.

A NEW RECORD

Suter may hold the record for the longest distance traveled by anyone picked up by a tornado who lived to tell about it: 1,307 feet (398 meters).

"I've never heard of anyone going that far in a tornado and surviving," tornado researcher Tom Grazulis said. "In more than forty thousand reports about tornadoes, I've only found one person who was carried more than a mile. But he **died**."

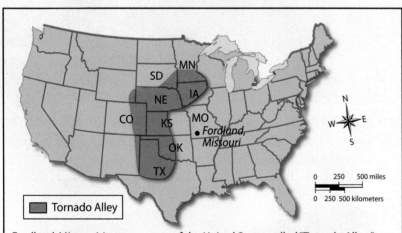

Tornado Alley

Fordland, Missouri, is near an area of the United States called "Tornado Alley." Tornado Alley gets more tornadoes than anywhere else in the world.

© NGSP & HB

Key Vocabulary
injured *adjective*, hurt
die *verb*, to stop living

In Other Words
lost consciousness fell into a deep sleep
collapsing falling
150-mile-per-hour 241-kilometer-per-hour
raging blackness dark, wild wind
dazed not sure what had happened

Interact with the Text

4. Photos and Captions

If you wanted to add a photo to go with this part of the text, what could the photo show?

_____

_____

_____

_____

5. Maps and Captions

Reread the text on page 125. Where does Suter live?

_____

_____

Read the caption for the map. Is Suter's hometown part of "Tornado Alley"?

_____

What does this tell you about tornadoes?

Tornadoes _____

_____

_____

6. Maps and Captions

Read the text. Underline the words that describe how Suter was when he woke up.

Look at the map. Then read the caption. What does the broken red line show?

It shows _____

_____.

Connect the map and the text. What do they help you understand about Suter's survival?

The text says that when Suter woke up, he was

_____

_____

_____.

The map shows that

_____

_____

_____.

I think Suter survived because he was

_____

_____

_____.

When Suter woke up, he **was confused**. There was blood pouring down his face from the cut in his head. "Everything was gone. I could see **debris** everywhere," he said.

Suter was **barefoot** and soaking wet from rain. He started looking for help. A neighbor found Suter at his door. He wrapped Suter in a blanket. Then the neighbor called his brother, who drove Suter back to see the **damage**.

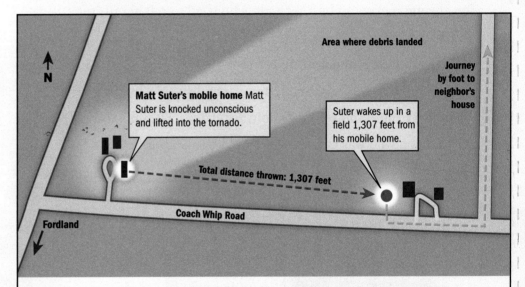

Matt Suter survived being sucked up by a tornado and thrown 1,307 feet (almost five soccer fields) away. He may have set a new record for distance traveled by a tornado survivor.

Key Vocabulary
damage *noun*, harm or hurt

In Other Words
was confused did not know what had happened
debris pieces of my house
barefoot not wearing shoes

Tornado survivor Matt Suter stands in front of what remains of his home.

"The only thing left is the deck I'd been building for my grandma," Suter said. "Everything else is in the field or in the trees."

Suter's physician, Dr. Ron Buening, said that Suter will **recover** from his injuries. "He was the luckiest man on earth," Buening said.

Interact with the Text

7. Photos and Captions

What are the objects in the bottom right corner of the photo? How do you know?

The objects are _____

_____

_____.

I know this because _____

_____

_____.

8. Photos and Captions

What is in the photo directly behind Matt Suter? Underline the words in the text that explain.

In the photo, the structure

behind Suter is _____

_____

_____.

AFTER THE STORM

Suter plans to help his grandmother rebuild her home. After he graduates, he wants to join the Marines.

As for being a tornado survivor? "I've always wanted to see a tornado," he said. "But I sure didn't want to be in one." ❖

Selection Review Tornado Survivor Called "the Luckiest Man on Earth"

A. Make a list of the photos and maps in this article. Use the photos, the maps, the captions, and the text to make notes about Suter's experience.

Page	Description of Photo or Map	What It Helps Me Understand
____	a large tornado	Tornadoes are very big and scary.
127	_____	Suter lives _____ _____.
128	map that shows how far away the debris _____, how far Suter was _____, and where he _____ afterwards	These distances are _____.
129	_____ _____	_____ _____

B. Dr. Buening thinks that Suter was lucky. Do you agree or disagree? Why? Complete the sentence.

> I _____ that Suter was lucky because _____
>
> _____.

Reflect and Assess

WRITING: Write About Literature

A. What helps people survive? Plan your writing. Read each statement about what helped Noni and Matt Suter survive. Do you agree or disagree with the statement? Mark your opinion with an *X*.

Statement	Agree	Disagree
Matt Suter survived because he stayed calm.		
Noni survived because he made a knife.		
Matt Suter survived because he was young and strong.		
Noni survived because he was good to his dog.		
Matt Suter survived because he looked for help.		
Noni survived because he waited for help to arrive.		

B. Write a Survival Guide. What should people remember when they face fear and danger? Read the student model.

Student Model

> To survive danger, you need to stay calm and think about how to get help. If you remember to use what you have, you will be more likely to survive. That is the most important thing.

C. Now write your own Survival Guide. Use ideas from the chart above.

Paragraph Organizer

To survive danger, you need _____.

If you remember _____, you will be more likely

to survive. That is the most important thing.

Integrate the Language Arts

VOCABULARY STUDY: Use a Dictionary

When you come to a word you do not know, use a dictionary to learn more about the word. Follow these steps.

- Use guide words to find the right page. Then find the word.
- Read the pronunciation. Say the word.
- Learn the part of speech of the word.
- Read the definition.
- Reread the word in the text. Use the meaning of the word to unlock the meaning of the text.

A. Read the text and the dictionary entry.

> The food was gone, and Noni and Nimuk were lost in the <u>wilderness</u>.

Dictionary

> wife • will

> **wilderness**   (wil-dur-nus) *noun*   an area or region not used often by people

B. Answer questions about the word *wilderness*.

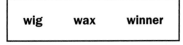

wig   wax   winner

1. Look at the guide words on the dictionary page. Which word in the box may be on the same page as *wilderness*? Circle it.

2. Look at the pronunciation. Say *wilderness* aloud. How many parts is the word divided into? _____

3. What part of speech is *wilderness*? _____

4. Explain in your own words what wilderness is. _____
_____

5. Reread the sentence about Noni and Nimuk. Think about the story. Explain why the word *wilderness* is important in this sentence.
_____
_____

LITERARY ANALYSIS: Literary Element: Plot

The plot is the order of action in a story. It is all the things that happen from the beginning to the end. You can use a Plot Diagram to describe the plot of a story.

A. Reread "Two Were Left." Complete the sentences.

1. **Problem:** _____ and his dog, _____, are alone. They have not eaten for three days. They are _____.

2. **Events:** Noni decides to kill Nimuk for food. Noni makes a _____. But Noni cannot kill Nimuk. He throws the _____ away. Noni gets scared when Nimuk _____ at him. He thinks Nimuk will kill him. Instead, Nimuk _____ Noni.

3. **Turning Point:** A pilot sees the shining _____ that Noni made.

4. **Solution:** The pilot finds _____.

B. Now use your answers to complete the Plot Diagram for "Two Were Left."

Plot Diagram

② **Middle**
Turning Point: _____

_____

Events:

_____

_____

_____

_____

③ **End**
Solution: _____

_____

① **Beginning**
Problem: _____

_____

Prepare to Read
▶ Surviving Katrina
▶ Test Your Survival Skills

Key Vocabulary

Circle a number to rate how well you know each word. Mark an *X* next to the correct definition to check your understanding. Then write a definition.

Rating Scale

1 I do not know this word.	**2** I am not sure of the word's meaning.	**3** I know this word. I can teach the word to someone else.

Key Word	Check Your Understanding	Deepen Your Understanding
① choice (**chois**) *noun* Rating: 1 2 3	☐ when you explain something ☐ when you pick something	My definition: _____ _____ _____
② disaster (di-**zas**-tur) *noun* Rating: 1 2 3	☐ an event that helps people, animals, or things ☐ an event that harms people, animals, or things	My definition: _____ _____ _____
③ neighbor (**nā**-bur) *noun* Rating: 1 2 3	☐ someone who lives near you ☐ someone who lives far from you	My definition: _____ _____ _____
④ obstacle (**ob**-sti-kul) *noun* Rating: 1 2 3	☐ something that stops you ☐ something that you share	My definition: _____ _____ _____

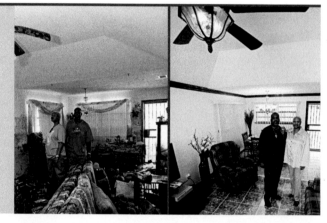

Every **victim** was a **stranger** to me, but I still wanted to help. ▶

Key Word	Check Your Understanding	Deepen Your Understanding
5 safety (**sāf**-tē) *noun* Rating: **1 2 3**	☐ a place where you cannot be hurt ☐ a place where you get hurt	My definition: _____ _____ _____
6 save (**sāv**) *verb* Rating: **1 2 3**	☐ to stop someone or something from being angry ☐ to stop someone or something from being hurt or destroyed	My definition: _____ _____ _____
7 stranger (**strān**-jur) *noun* Rating: **1 2 3**	☐ someone you do not know ☐ someone you know	My definition: _____ _____ _____
8 victim (**vik**-tum) *noun* Rating: **1 2 3**	☐ a person who was hurt ☐ a person who is helpful	My definition: _____ _____ _____

READING STRATEGY: Plan and Monitor

Reading Strategy
Plan and Monitor

HOW TO PREVIEW AND SET A PURPOSE

1. Look quickly at the text. Notice headings, pictures, and other visuals.

2. Look at the title and cover. Ask, "What is the text about?"

3. Read the first few sentences. Think some more on what the text is about.

4. Ask, "What do I want to find out?" Your answer is your purpose for reading.

A. Read the heading and text. Look at the picture.

Look Into the Text

PREVIEW

The photo and the text explain that
_____
_____
_____
_____ .

SET A PURPOSE

I'll read on to find out _____
_____
_____
_____ .

A Disaster

Then Hurricane Katrina struck. Courtney's neighborhood was flooded. There was no electricity. People had no food or clean water. The flood waters were knee high. "Man, we have to do something to get out of here," Courtney told his friends.

B. Now preview and set a purpose for your reading. Complete the thought bubbles above to show your thinking.

Selection Review Surviving Katrina

EQ **What Does It Take to Survive?**
Find out how creative thinking can help people survive.

A. In "Surviving Katrina," you read how Courtney Miles helped his neighbors survive. Look back at the section headings and the pictures. What purpose did you set for each section? What did you learn? Complete the chart.

Section Heading	My Purpose	What I Learned
A Troubled Past	I wanted to know about Courtney's past.	I learned that he was on his own with no home, food, or money.
A Disaster	I wanted to know _____ _____ _____	I learned that he _____ _____ _____
The Road to Safety	I wanted to know _____ _____ _____	I learned that he _____ _____ _____
A New Life	I wanted to know _____ _____ _____	I learned that _____ _____ _____

B. Answer the questions. Use your chart to help you.

1. What creative idea did Courtney have? _____
_____

2. What choice did Courtney make in order to put his idea into action? _____
_____

3. Why do you think Courtney's experience during Hurricane Katrina changed his life?
_____
_____

Before Reading Test Your Survival Skills

READING STRATEGY: Plan and Monitor

Reading Strategy
Plan and Monitor

HOW TO CLARIFY IDEAS

1. Stop reading after difficult sentences or paragraphs. Ask yourself, "What is the writer saying?" Explain the text to yourself in your own words. If you still do not understand, reread those sections.

2. If rereading doesn't help you, read on. You might find information later in the text that will help you understand.

3. Read at the right speed. You might need to read some texts more slowly.

A. Read the text and clarify ideas. Complete the thought bubbles.

Look Into the Text

CHALLENGE 2

WISDOM TEETH

A plane crashed into a mountain. The pilot and his elderly passenger were badly hurt. They had no food or water. The pilot finally found a stream. But his hands were very burned. He could not scoop up the water.

The passenger wore dentures, or false teeth. The pilot removed the dentures and turned them upside down. He used them as a cup to lift water from the stream.

The survivor found _____ _____, but he could not _____ _____.

He used the dentures like a _____.

B. Now think about how you read the text. Circle your answer.

1. I read (too quickly/too slowly/at the right speed).

2. I (never/sometimes/often) reread parts of the text.

3. I (never/sometimes/often) stopped after difficult sentences or paragraphs.

Connect Across Texts

In "Surviving Katrina," you learned how Courtney Miles survived a **disaster**. Read this magazine article to see how you could survive a disaster.

TEST YOUR SURVIVAL SKILLS

BY NICK D'ALTO
Odyssey, December 1, 2005
ILLUSTRATIONS BY CHRIS VALLO

Survival experts often say that the way you think might be your most important survival tool. In an emergency, you need to be able to see ordinary things in extraordinary ways. Experts call this "**lateral thinking**."

Here are two true survival stories. Read about each situation. Then brainstorm. How did each survivor "think" his or her way out of **danger**?

CHALLENGE 1

CREDIT THESE GUYS WITH GENIUS

A boat sank. Three friends were stuck on an island. Their radio was gone. Their cell phone wouldn't work. Yet they rescued themselves by using a credit card. How was it possible?

Key Vocabulary

disaster *noun*, an event that harms a lot of people, animals, or things

In Other Words

lateral thinking thinking in new and different ways

danger the situation that could harm the survivor

Interact with the Text

1. Preview and Set a Purpose

Preview this article by reading the title and the headings. What do you think the article is about? What do you think you will find out?

I think the article is about

_____

_____ .

I think I will find out

_____

_____ .

2. Clarify Ideas

Read the first paragraph. Underline the words that explain the idea of "lateral thinking."

Explain this idea in your own words.

"Lateral thinking" means

_____

_____

_____ .

3. Clarify Ideas

Underline the words that describe how a credit card looks.

Circle the words that tell how friends used the credit card to signal the plane.

Explain how the credit card worked as a signal.

People in the plane saw _____

_____

_____ .

4. Clarify Ideas

Circle the two things the friends used to make the signal stronger.

If the plane were 200 miles away, could the pilot see the signal? If you don't know the answer, reread the text.

Reflected sunlight can be spotted _____ miles away. At 200 miles away, the pilot probably (can/ cannot) see the signal because _____

_____

_____ .

ANSWER

That credit card was valuable—but only if you think laterally. Credit cards are made from plastic. They're usually shiny on one side. One friend used the credit card to reflect sunlight. The flashes were noticed by a passing plane. (Sometimes, reflected sunlight can be spotted 100 miles, or 160 kilometers, away.)

At first, the card didn't reflect strongly enough. So the friends **dunked** the card in sea water. This made it shinier. Then they used their fingers to help aim the signal as a plane flew overhead.

The lesson? When they looked at the credit card, the friends saw more than just a useless piece of plastic. And then they turned their worst **obstacles**—water and the blazing sun—into a way to improve their plan for survival.

Key Vocabulary
obstacle *noun*, something that stops you from doing what you want to do

In Other Words
dunked put

CHALLENGE 2

WISDOM TEETH

A plane crashed into a mountain. The pilot and **his elderly passenger** were badly hurt. They had no food or water. The pilot finally found a **stream**. But his hands were very burned. He could not **scoop up** the water. The passenger was too weak to reach the stream. Yet the passenger's age helped them get water. Can you guess how?

ANSWER

It's **gross**. The passenger wore dentures, or false teeth. The pilot removed the dentures and turned them upside down. He used them as a cup to lift water from the stream. Now he and the passenger could drink. **Disgusting**? You do what you have to do to survive.

5. Clarify Ideas

Read Challenge 2. Explain the problem in your own words.

The pilot and his passenger

could not _____

_____ , because

_____

_____

_____

_____ .

6. Clarify Ideas

Read the answer to the challenge. Underline the sentences that tell what the pilot did to solve the problem.

Break the sentences into three steps to clarify ideas. Try to use your own words to retell the steps.

Step 1: The pilot _____

_____ .

Step 2: He _____

_____ .

Step 3: He used them ____

_____ .

In Other Words
his elderly passenger the old person on the plane
stream small river
scoop up use his hands to pick up
gross awful
Disgusting Awful

7. Clarify Ideas

What does the writer mean by "now it's your turn"? Read on. Then explain in your own words what this section is about.

The writer means that

_____

_____

_____ .

NOW IT'S YOUR TURN!

Your only tool is a garbage bag. How many survival uses for it can you think of? Could you make a **poncho** to keep dry? A **kite** to call **rescuers**? **A stretcher to move** the injured? Use lateral thinking. How many possible uses can you think of? ❖

In Other Words
poncho rain coat
kite flying object
rescuers people who can help you
A stretcher to move An object to carry

Selection Review   Test Your Survival Skills

A. Explain what happened to the people in the article. Complete the chart.

Challenge 1	Challenge 2
Three friends were stranded on an island. They used a _____ to _____ .	A pilot survived a plane crash, but his hands were _____ . He used _____ to get _____ .

B. Use your notes to clarify the idea of "lateral thinking."

"Lateral thinking" means _____ .

Reflect and Assess

WRITING: Write About Literature

A. Plan your writing. Why do strangers help each other during a disaster?
List some additional reasons.

Possible Reasons
• People are mostly good.
• They are too scared not to help.
• _____
• _____

B. Now write about your own opinion. Find examples from the selections to
support your opinion.

1. State Opinion	2. Support Opinion
I think strangers help each other because _____ _____ _____ .	I read that _____ _____ _____ .

C. Finish this paragraph to express your opinion. Explain why people help
each other in a disaster. Use your notes.

Paragraph Organizer

　　　In my opinion, people help each other in a disaster because _____

_____. In "Surviving Katrina," Courtney Miles

_____. This shows that he

_____. In "Test Your Survival Skills,"

a survivor of a plane crash _____. He did this

because he wanted to _____. These examples

clearly show that _____.

Integrate the Language Arts

VOCABULARY STUDY: Multiple-Meaning Words

Many English words have more than one meaning. The meanings are numbered in the dictionary. The dictionary entry often shows different parts of speech.

> **start**   (**start**) *verb*   **1** : to begin to do something or go somewhere   *noun*   **2** : the place where a game or a race begins

A. Read the sentence about Courtney Miles. Then answer the questions.

"This fall, he will start college."

1. In this sentence, the word *start* is a (**noun/verb**).

2. Use the meaning of the word to restate the sentence. _____

_____

B. Read each sentence and dictionary entry. Find the meaning that fits the sentence. Circle the number of the meaning that fits.

3. "Courtney Miles is a successful young <u>man</u>."

> **man**   (**man**) *noun*   **1** : a grown-up person who is male   *verb*   **2** : to have the people needed to make something work

4. "This <u>fall</u>, he will start college."

> **fall**   (**fol**) *verb*   **1** : to drop from a higher place to a lower place   *noun*   **2** : the time of year between summer and winter

5. "Along the way, strangers begged for a <u>ride</u>."

> **ride**   (**rīd**) *verb*   **1** : to travel in a vehicle or on an animal   *noun*   **2** : the act of traveling in a vehicle or on an animal

LITERARY ANALYSIS: Compare Fiction and Nonfiction

Stories about imaginary people, places, things, and events are called fiction. Texts that give information about real people, places, things, and events are called nonfiction.

A. Review "Two Were Left" and "Surviving Katrina." Then fill in the answers below. Write *fiction*, *nonfiction*, or *both*.

1. Can include illustrations: _____both_____

2. Can include chapters: _____

3. Can include photographs and captions: _____

4. About imaginary people: _____

5. Can have a plot: _____

B. Use your answers to complete the Venn Diagram.

Venn Diagram

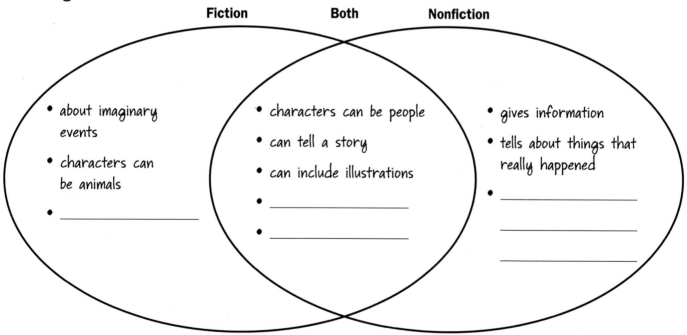

Fiction   Both   Nonfiction

- about imaginary events
- characters can be animals
- _____

- characters can be people
- can tell a story
- can include illustrations
- _____
- _____

- gives information
- tells about things that really happened
- _____
  _____
  _____

Prepare to Read

▶ **Fight or Flight? What Your Body Knows About Survival**
▶ **Survivor Rulon Gardner: Hardheaded**

Key Vocabulary

Circle a number to rate how well you know each word. Circle the word that completes the sentence to check your understanding. Then complete the sentences.

Rating Scale

1 I do not know this word.	**2** I am not sure of the word's meaning.	**3** I know this word. I can teach the word to someone else.

Key Word	Check Your Understanding	Deepen Your Understanding
❶ blood vessel (**blud ve**-sul) *noun* Rating: 1 2 3	A **blood vessel** is a _____. tube bone	A **blood vessel** is important because _____ _____ _____.
❷ circumstances (**sur**-kum-stans-uz) *noun* Rating: 1 2 3	**Circumstances** are the facts or details of a _____. sport situation	The **circumstances** that lead to good grades include _____ _____.
❸ danger (**dān**-jur) *noun* Rating: 1 2 3	**Danger** is the possibility of _____. joy harm	When I see **danger** near me, I _____ _____ _____.
❹ energy (**e**-nur-jē) *noun* Rating: 1 2 3	**Energy** is the ability to be _____. active tough	You need a lot of **energy** to play a sport, because you have to _____ _____.

Physical activity might make you perspire. ▶

Key Word	Check Your Understanding	Deepen Your Understanding
5 escape (is-**kāp**) *verb* Rating: 1 2 3	To **escape** is to _____ . go to get away	Most people would want to **escape** from _____ _____ _____ .
6 perspire (pur-**spīr**) *verb* Rating: 1 2 3	If you **perspire**, you _____ . run sweat	People might **perspire** when they _____ _____ _____ .
7 physical (**fi**-zi-kul) *adjective* Rating: 1 2 3	If something is **physical**, it is about the _____ . body truth	In **physical** education class, students _____ _____ _____ .
8 system (**sis**-tum) *noun* Rating: 1 2 3	A **system** is a group of _____ . sports parts	A computer **system** includes a monitor and _____ _____ _____ _____ .

Before Reading Fight or Flight? What Your Body Knows About Survival

READING STRATEGY: Plan and Monitor

HOW TO CLARIFY VOCABULARY

1. Read the text. Stop if you see a word you don't know. Ask, "Have I seen the word before? What do I already know about it?" Look at the word parts.

2. If you still do not understand the word, reread the sentence. Try to find clues to predict the word's meaning.

3. If you still do not understand, read on. The meaning may become clearer in the text you read later.

4. Confirm your prediction by looking up the word in a dictionary.

A. Read the text. Notice the underlined words. Complete the sentence in the thought bubble.

Look Into the Text

Luckily for you, your body has weapons that take over when you sense danger. When you see the tiger, your hypothalamus sends a message through the circulatory system to parts of your body.

I don't know the word "hypothalamus."
I will _____
_____
_____ .

B. Reread the text. Clarify the meaning of the underlined words. Use a dictionary to confirm your predictions. Complete the chart.

Word or Phrase	Clue in Text	What I Predict Is the Meaning	Meaning from Dictionary
hypothalamus	"When you see the tiger, your hypothalamus sends a message"	body part that sends messages	the part of the brain that produces hormones that control fear, anger, hunger, and thirst
circulatory system			

Selection Review Fight or Flight? What Your Body Knows About Survival

EQ **What Does It Take to Survive?**
Explore how the body and mind work together for survival.

A. In "Fight or Flight?" you learned what the body does in survival situations. Reread the text. Find three words that are new to you. Add them to the chart below. Then complete the chart.

Word or Phrase	Clue in Text	What I Predict Is the Meaning	Meaning from Dictionary
adrenal glands	"release special chemicals"	parts of the body that _____ _____	glands that produce hormones that prepare the body to react to danger
_____	_____	_____ _____	_____ _____ _____
_____	_____	_____ _____	_____ _____ _____
_____	_____	_____ _____	_____ _____ _____

B. Use your chart to answer the questions.

1. What do the adrenal glands do when someone is in danger?

   The adrenal glands _____ .

2. How does this help someone face danger?

   It helps someone face danger because _____

   _____ .

3. How does the body respond to keep someone from bleeding to death from a small cut?

   Tiny blood vessels called _____ get smaller, which makes _____ .

4. Can you jump higher when you're afraid? Why or why not?

   _____

Before Reading Survivor Rulon Gardner: Hardheaded

© NGSP & HB

TEXT STRUCTURE: Sequence

HOW TO IDENTIFY SEQUENCE

1. Read the text. Look for words related to time, such as *when, first, next,* and *later.*

2. Write the events in a **Sequence Chart**.

3. Use your Sequence Chart to keep track of the order of events.

A. Read the text. Think about the sequence of events in Rulon Gardner's life.

Look Into the Text

In 2000 he won the Olympic gold medal for wrestling. This was a great show of strength.

But in 2002, Gardner was stranded in the freezing wilderness. His physical strength could not help him. He lost a toe, but he survived. Then, in the winter of 2007, Gardner's plane crashed into a lake. How did he and his friends survive? Gardner explains.

B. Now complete the Sequence Chart.

Sequence Chart

Event 1	Event 2	Event 3
In _____, he won an Olympic gold medal.	In _____, he was lost in the wilderness.	In _____, he survived a plane crash.

Connect Across Texts

In "Fight or Flight?" you learned what your body does automatically to survive. In this magazine profile, an Olympic champion tells what he has learned about survival.

Survivor Rulon Gardner: Hardheaded

by Andrea Minarcek
National Geographic Adventure

Many believe that **physical** strength is important to survival. But is survival just about muscles? Take Rulon Gardner. In 2000 he won the Olympic gold medal for wrestling. This was a great show of strength.

But in 2002, Gardner was stranded in the freezing **wilderness**. His physical strength could not help him. He lost a toe, but he survived. Then, in the winter of 2007, Gardner's plane crashed into a lake. How did he and his friends survive? Gardner explains.

Key Vocabulary
physical *adjective*, about the body

In Other Words
wilderness place far from people and things people build

Interact with the Text

1. Sequence
Circle dates and time words that signal the main events in Rulon's life. What event happened in each year?

Event 1: In 2000, _____

_____

_____.

Event 2: In _____

_____

_____

_____.

Event 3: _____

_____

Lake Powell, Utah

2. Sequence

What is the first event in the sequence that Rulon describes on this page?

Event 1: Rulon's plane struck

_____

Underline the sentence that describes what Rulon did as soon as he found himself in the water. Complete Event 2.

Event 2: Rulon started to

_____

3. Sequence

Circle the words that describe what Rulon did when he got to the shore. Complete Event 3.

Event 3: Rulon _____

_____

_____

Take it one step at a time. "When the plane struck Lake Powell, the water was freezing. My two friends and I were two miles from shore. I'm not a great swimmer. I started **doing the backstroke**, slowly. I kept telling myself, 'Just make it to land.' That was my goal. Anything beyond that, I couldn't think about. It was too much."

Accept your circumstances. "When I got to shore, I thought, 'If this isn't a dream, then I'll feel the sand. I'll feel the sun's warmth. I'll feel the heat.' I lay there for a while. But after everything I've been through, I knew I had to make myself act. I couldn't get paralyzed by fear."

Key Vocabulary
circumstances *noun*, facts or details of a situation

In Other Words
doing the backstroke
swimming on my back

© NGSP & HB

Make a game plan. "When I was wrestling, I'd work through what was about to happen. Having **positive mental imagery** beforehand gives you a plot to follow. That's what I did as soon as I got to shore."

Sit tight. "We were miles from anyone and anything. We realized the best thing to do was prepare for the night. It was **twenty-five degrees**. We tried to bask in the sun and dry our clothes. The last thing we could do was fall asleep. So we did anything and everything to keep awake."

Hypothermia

When Rulon Gardner was fighting for his life in Lake Powell, the water was freezing. His body temperature dropped below normal **(98.6° F)**. This is called hypothermia.

What are the signs of hypothermia?

- Intense **shivering**
- Slow movement and confusion
- Lips, ears, fingers, and toes can turn blue

How can hypothermia be prevented?

Wearing the right clothing can help prevent hypothermia. In the water, wear a wet suit or dry suit to keep heat in your body. On land, wear a hat to keep your head warm. Since most heat is lost through your head, this is a very important step.

In Other Words
positive mental imagery pictures in your head about good things that can happen
Sit tight. Don't move.
shivering uncontrolled body shaking

twenty-five degrees –3° Celsius
98.6°F 37° Celsius

4. Sequence
What did Rulon do after he thought for a while? Complete Event 4.

Event 4: After he thought for a while, Rulon _____

_____

5. Sequence
Underline the words that tell what Rulon and his friends did to plan for the night. Complete Event 5.

Event 5: They dried their clothes and _____

_____

6. Clarify Vocabulary
Based on the text, what do you think *intense* means? Use a dictionary to confirm your prediction. Complete this sentence to show the meaning.

Someone who has intense shivering is _____

Be glad for what you've got.

"If I started with nine lives, I think I have about two left. But, hey, that'll be enough to get me through." ❖

Interact with the Text

7. Clarify Vocabulary

What does the expression "to have nine lives" mean? Look for clues. Then make a prediction. Confirm your prediction.

I predict that it means
_____
_____
_____

Selection Review Survivor Rulon Gardner: Hardheaded

A. Think about the sequence of events in Rulon Gardner's survival story. Complete the Sequence Chart.

Sequence Chart

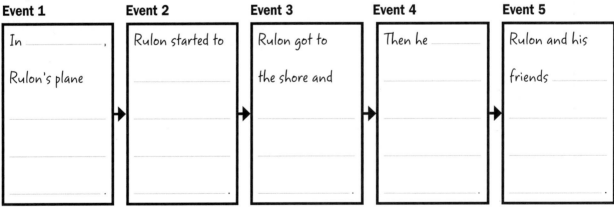

Event 1	Event 2	Event 3	Event 4	Event 5
In _____, Rulon's plane	Rulon started to	Rulon got to the shore and	Then he	Rulon and his friends

B. Reread your Sequence Chart. What do you think happened to Rulon and his friends after Event 5? Write your ideas below.

After Rulon and his friends stayed awake all night, they probably _____
_____.

Reflect and Assess

WRITING: Write About Literature

A. Plan your writing. Read the opinion statement.

> Physical strength is more important for survival than mental strength.

Do you agree or disagree? Think about the selections you read. Find examples that support your opinion. Complete the sentences in the chart.

1. State Opinion	2. Support Opinion
I think that _____ strength is more important than _____ strength.	I think this because I read that _____ _____.

B. Now express your opinion. Explain whether physical strength or mental strength is more important for survival. Use your notes.

Paragraph Organizer

In my opinion, _____ strength is more important than _____ strength. I think this because of what I read in "Survivor Rulon Gardner: Hardheaded." Rulon survived the plane crash because _____ _____. I also have this opinion because of _____. I learned that _____ _____. This tells me that _____ _____. These examples clearly show that what matters most for survival is _____ strength.

Integrate the Language Arts

▶ **Fight or Flight? What Your Body Knows About Survival**
▶ **Survivor Rulon Gardner: Hardheaded**

VOCABULARY STUDY: Multiple-Meaning Words

Many English words have more than one meaning. The meanings are numbered in the dictionary. The dictionary entry often shows different parts of speech.

> **show** (shō) *verb* **1** : to let people see something
> *noun* **2** : something that people can see

A. Read the sentence about Rulon Gardner. Then answer the questions.

"This was a great show of strength."

1. In this sentence, the word *show* is a **(noun / verb)**.

2. Use the meaning of *show* to restate the sentence in your own words.

_____

B. Read each sentence and dictionary entry. Find the meaning that fits the sentence. Circle the number of the meaning that fits.

3. "He lost a <u>toe</u>, but he survived."

> **toe** (tō) *noun* **1** : part of the foot   *verb* **2** : to touch or kick with the tip of the foot

4. "Then, in the winter of 2007, Gardner's plane <u>crashed</u> into a lake."

> **crash** (krash) *verb* **1** : to smash into something
> *noun* **2** : a loud noise

5. "'I knew I had to make myself <u>act</u>.'"

> **act** (akt) *noun* **1** : something that is done   *verb* **2** : to do something   *verb* **3** : to perform in a play

6. "'That's what I did as soon as I got to <u>shore</u>.'"

> **shore** (shōr) *noun* **1** : land next to a river, lake, or ocean
> *verb* **2** : to support something so it keeps standing

LISTENING AND SPEAKING: Act It Out

Work with two partners. Use the information in the article. Imagine what Rulon and his two friends said to each other when they reached the shore. Complete the script. Then act it out with your partners.

RULON. We did it! We're alive!

FRIEND 1. We were swimming for so long. And the water was so cold.

FRIEND 2. [*shaking*] I know. I'm freezing.

RULON. [*to* FRIEND 1] You're shivering. You have hypothermia. You need to get warm. Let's turn toward the sun and try to get warm.

FRIEND 2. How cold do you think it is?

FRIEND 1. I think it's about twenty-five degrees. In this weather, we could freeze to death. I'm so afraid. What are we going to do? I don't even know where we are!

RULON. Look, we can't let our fear control us. We have to be calm and accept our circumstances.

FRIEND 2. But the sun is almost down. It will be night soon. We can't go anywhere in the dark. What are we going to do?

RULON. Let's make a game plan. When I was wrestling, I made a game plan before every match.

FRIEND 1. How will that help us?

RULON. If we make a plan for the night, then we will know how to act when things get difficult. We will have pictures in our minds about how we want things to happen.

FRIEND 2. OK. Let's make a plan.

RULON. If we go to sleep, we could die of hypothermia. We cannot go to sleep.

FRIEND 1. _____

FRIEND 2. _____

RULON. _____

Vocabulary Review

A. Study each picture. Circle the word that completes the sentence.

1.

The storm did a lot of **(damage /
circumstances)** to the chair.

2.

A lion is a **(weak / powerful)** animal.

3.

(Fear / Safety) is the feeling you get
when you are afraid or scared.

4.
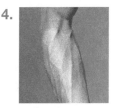

The **(instinct / blood vessel)** carries
blood from place to place.

B. Complete the chart below by adding the following words to the
correct column.

die   neighbor   recover   stranger   victim

escape   perspire   save   survive

Words That Name Actions	Words That Name People
die	neighbor

Unit 4 Vocabulary

blood vessel	defenseless	escape	obstacle	safety	victim
choice	die	fear	perspire	save	weak
circumstances	disaster	injured	physical	stranger	
damage	emergency	instinct	powerful	survive	
danger	energy	neighbor	recover	system	

C. Read each sentence. Circle the word that completes the sentence correctly.

1. My mom is a doctor. She knows what to do in an
(**emergency / obstacle**).

2. Ray is a (**weak / powerful**) soccer player. He is our team captain.

3. What was your (**victim / choice**) for breakfast—eggs or cereal?

4. The brain is a very important part of your nervous
(**neighbor / system**).

5. The nurse treated Luisa's (**injured / powerful**) arm.

6. Without their mother, the baby birds were (**powerful / defenseless**).

7. The flood was a (**disaster / stranger**) for everyone who lives in
the valley.

8. I smelled smoke. I knew that we were in (**circumstances / danger**) if
the fire came closer.

9. The small car accident created a big (**obstacle / blood vessel**) for the
other cars on the road.

10. I need a lot of (**fear / energy**) to run the race.

Unit Vocabulary

Circle a number to rate how well you know each word. Circle the word that completes the sentence to check your understanding. Then write a definition.

▲ Baseball is a **popular** sport at my school.

Key Word	Check Your Understanding	Deepen Your Understanding
❶ **believe** (bu-**lēv**) *verb* **Rating: 1 2 3**	When you **believe** a story, you think it is _____. **true false**	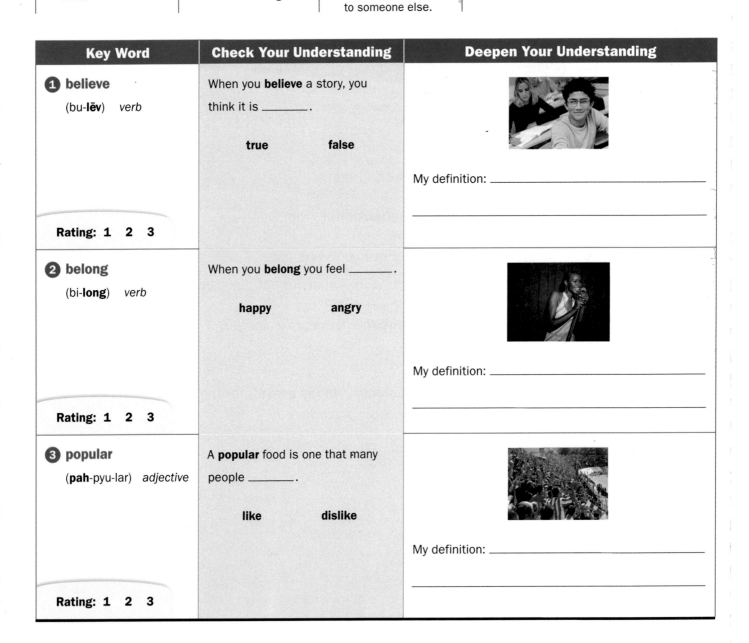 My definition: _____ _____
❷ **belong** (bi-**long**) *verb* **Rating: 1 2 3**	When you **belong** you feel _____. **happy angry**	My definition: _____ _____
❸ **popular** (**pah**-pyu-lar) *adjective* **Rating: 1 2 3**	A **popular** food is one that many people _____. **like dislike**	My definition: _____ _____

Vocabulary Workshop

Use Context Clues

There are different kinds of context clues.

TYPE OF CLUE	DESCRIPTION	SIGNAL WORDS
Definition clue	Explains what the word means	*is, are, was, refers to, means*
Restatement clue	Gives the meaning in a different way, usually after a comma	*or*
Example clue	Gives an example of what the word means	*such as, for example, including*
Synonym clue	Gives a word or phrase that means almost the same thing	*like, also*
Antonym clue	Gives a word or phrase that means the opposite	*but, unlike*

When you read, you may find a word you do not know. Use context clues to figure out the word's meaning.

- Reread the words nearby. Look for signal words.
- Predict what the word means.
- Try out the predicted meaning to see if it makes sense.

Practice Using Context Clues

Read the paragraph. Circle each signal word that helps you figure out the meaning of the underlined words.

Ricardo is a senior, which means he's in his final year of high school. He is an eccentric, or unusual, person. He wears interesting outfits, such as bright shirts, large hats, and bowling shoes. Ricardo has an elaborate style, but his best friend's style is simple. In real friendships, differences in style are insignificant, or not important.

I predict that a "senior" is someone in his or her final year of high school.

Put the Strategy to Use

Use context clues to predict the meaning of each word. Check that the meaning makes sense.

1. eccentric _____

2. outfits _____

3. elaborate _____

4. insignificant _____

Prepare to Read

▶ Frijoles
▶ The Jay and the Peacocks

Key Vocabulary

Circle a number to rate how well you know each word. Circle *yes* or *no* to check your understanding. Then complete the sentences.

Rating Scale		
1 I do not know this word.	**2** I am not sure of the word's meaning.	**3** I know this word. I can teach the word to someone else.

Key Word	Check Your Understanding	Deepen Your Understanding
❶ agreement (u-**grē**-munt) *noun* Rating: 1 2 3	People fight when they are in **agreement**. Yes No	Our teacher smiles in agreement when we _____
❷ alone (u-**lōn**) *adverb* Rating: 1 2 3	Jason likes to study **alone** with all his friends. Yes No	People usually like to be alone when they are _____
❸ arrive (u-**rīv**) *verb* Rating: 1 2 3	I take my coat off when I **arrive** at school. Yes No	When they arrive at the park, they _____
❹ exotic (ig-**zah**-tik) *adjective* Rating: 1 2 3	This bright red hat with feathers looks very **exotic**! Yes No	That fish is exotic because _____

When I **arrive** home from school, I like to be **alone**. ▶

Key Word	Check Your Understanding	Deepen Your Understanding
5 jealous (**je**-lus) *adjective* Rating: 1 2 3	Brian felt **jealous** when he saw Ed's new car. Yes No	Jealous people are sad because _____
6 ordinary (**or**-du-nair-ē) *adjective* Rating: 1 2 3	An ice cream sandwich is an **ordinary** lunch. Yes No	An example of ordinary clothing is _____
7 prepare (pri-**pair**) *verb* Rating: 1 2 3	Sophia will **prepare** for the math test after it is over. Yes No	Each morning, I prepare for school by _____
8 suggest (sug-**jest**) *verb* Rating: 1 2 3	Please **suggest** where we should go for lunch. Yes No	If a friend asks you which book to read, you might suggest _____

Before Reading Frijoles

READING STRATEGY: Make Connections

HOW TO MAKE CONNECTIONS

1. Read the text. Look for ideas that remind you of past experiences.

2. Ask, "Have I ever lived through anything like this?"

3. Write your connection on a self-stick note. Place it next to the text you are making a connection to.

4. Think about how the connection improves your understanding of the text.

A. Read the text and make a connection to a past experience. Write your connection on the self-stick note.

Look Into the Text

Tony returned from the kitchen with warm tortillas. . . . When Mitsuo bit into a tortilla, it crackled like a potato chip. He grunted and commented, "Interesting food."

Lincoln looked at Tony, and Tony looked back. Lincoln whispered, "We messed up. These tortillas are hard as rocks."

"Harder," Tony whispered back. "And the avocados ain't any good either. Five bucks apiece, man, and they're mostly black."

B. Write how your connection helps you understand the text.

_____

_____

_____

Selection Review Frijoles

 EQ **How Important Is It to Fit In?**
Think about when it is worth it to try to fit in.

A. In "Frijoles," you learned what it is like to try to fit in to a different culture. Use the chart to write connections from your own life. Then write how each connection helps you understand the text. Work with a partner and compare charts.

Connections Chart

The text says . . .	My connection . . .	This helps me because . . .
"But the Onos tried it all, smiled between bites, and drank their tea."	I remember one time _____ _____ _____ _____ _____.	I think the Onos _____ _____ _____ _____ _____.
"'We messed up,' Tony said. . . . 'Mexican food *really* is good. If we knew how to cook, you'd be in paradise.'"	One time, _____ _____ _____ _____ _____.	_____ _____ _____ _____ _____
"After an hour, they raced home. Knots of hunger were twisting in their stomachs. They arrived just in time."	In my experience, _____ _____ _____ _____ _____.	_____ _____ _____ _____ _____

B. Use the connections you made to answer the questions.

1. Why do Tony and Lincoln want to make a Mexican meal for the Onos?

_____

_____

2. How do Tony and Lincoln feel about the meal they cooked?

_____

_____

Before Reading The Jay and the Peacocks

Genre: Fable

HOW TO INTERPRET FABLES

1. As you read the story, think about people you know who act like the characters in the story.

2. Read the moral and think about how it connects to the story.

3. Decide how the story and its moral connect to your experiences.

A. Read the text. Think about the characters, the moral, and your experiences. Then complete the sentences in the thought bubbles.

Look Into the Text

Suddenly, the jay noticed something shiny lying along the path. The peacocks had dropped a few of their beautiful, long feathers. "I know what to do!" he said to himself. "I will make myself look like a peacock. Then I'll be as happy as they are."

*   *   *   *   *   *   *   *   *   *

MORAL: Be true to yourself, or you may lose the respect of others. ❖

Like the jay, some people
_____
_____
_____
_____ .

This reminds me of
_____
_____
_____ .

B. Now decide how the story and its moral connect to your experiences. Write your ideas. With a partner, discuss your connection.

_____

_____

_____

_____

Connect Across Texts

In "Frijoles," Tony and Lincoln do something special in order to fit in with the Ono family. In this fable, a bird does something special, too.

the Jay and the Peacocks

Based on the fable by Aesop • Illustrated by Keith Baker

One day, an **ordinary** jaybird flew by a farm. There he saw a **flock of peacocks**.

To the jay, the **exotic** peacocks seemed to have a perfect life. They had good food to eat from a birdfeeder. They had cool water to drink from a lovely **pond**. Their colorful feathers caught the sunlight like a rainbow. The peacocks seemed very **content**.

Interact with the Text

1. Interpret Fables

Circle the characters in the story. Who do you know that reminds you of one of these characters? Explain why.

_____

_____

_____

_____

Key Vocabulary
ordinary *adjective*, something you
  see, hear, or do often
exotic *adjective*, something you do
  not see, hear, or do often

In Other Words
flock of peacocks group of birds with long,
  colorful feathers
pond small lake
content happy

The jay felt **jealous**. He looked at his own plain feathers. He thought of his own **boring** home. He wished he could live like a peacock.

Suddenly, the jay noticed something shiny lying along the path. The peacocks had dropped a few of their beautiful, long feathers. "I know what to do!" he said to himself. "I will make myself look like a peacock. Then I'll be as happy as they are." He tied the feathers to his tail. He practiced walking **as proudly as** a peacock.

The next day, the jay joined the flock. Because of his beautiful new feathers, he **fit right in**. He ate the good food from the birdfeeder. He drank the cool water from the pond. As long as he kept his secret, the jay belonged to the flock. He finally felt content with his life.

Interact with the Text

2. Interpret Fables
Underline the word that tells how the jay felt. When did you ever feel that way?

_____

_____

_____

_____

_____

3. Make Connections
Connect the fable to your life. Complete the sentence.

The jay reminds me of

_____

_____

because he/she _____

_____

_____

Key Vocabulary
jealous *adjective*, unhappy because you want something that someone else has

In Other Words
boring uninteresting
as proudly as like he felt as good about himself as
fit right in seemed like the peacocks

4. Interpret Fables

Why were the other jays angry?

_____

_____

_____

_____

_____

5. Make Connections

Is the moral true for your life? Explain.

_____

_____

_____

_____

_____

One day, a strong wind blew through the farm. As the peacocks watched, **the jay's false feathers** blew away. The peacocks were **furious**.

"You are not one of us!" they cried. "It takes more than fine feathers to make a fine bird!" They **pecked** the jay over and over.

The jay decided to go back to his own kind. He flew across the field to his old home. But when he got there, the other jays were angry.

"We saw what you did," they said. "You wanted to be a peacock. Well, this is no home for you!" They chased him away, too.

The jay spent his life **alone** —without a friend and without a home.

MORAL: Be true to yourself, or you may lose the respect of others. ❖

Key Vocabulary
alone *adverb*, by yourself

In Other Words
the jay's false feathers the feathers the jay had tied to his tail
furious very angry
pecked bit
MORAL: The lesson you can learn from the story is this:

Selection Review The Jay and the Peacocks

A. What is the moral of this fable? Explain it in your own words.

_____

B. Connect the moral to the story and to your own experiences. Complete the chart.

Connect to the Story	Connect to Your Life
The jay was not true to himself because he _____.	I would not be true to myself if I _____.
The other jays lost respect for the jay because _____.	My friends might lose respect for me if _____.

Reflect and Assess

WRITING: Write About Literature

A. Plan your writing. What happens when someone tries to fit in? Review the two selections. Look for examples that help you answer the question. Use a Cause-and-Effect Chain to show how one event leads to another. Look at the student model.

Student Model

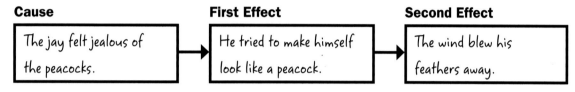

Cause	First Effect	Second Effect
The jay felt jealous of the peacocks.	He tried to make himself look like a peacock.	The wind blew his feathers away.

B. Make a Cause-and-Effect Chain to explore what happens when someone tries to fit in.

Cause-and-Effect Chain

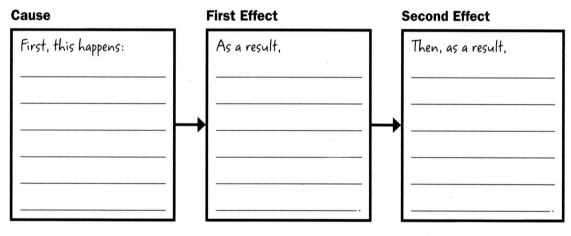

Cause	First Effect	Second Effect
First, this happens:	As a result,	Then, as a result,

C. Now write a summary of the events in your chain. Explain what happens when you try to fit in.

_____

_____

_____

_____

_____

Prepare to Read

▶ Cochlear Implants: Two Sides of the Story
▶ High School

Key Vocabulary

Circle a number to rate how well you know each word. Mark an *X* next to the correct definition to check your understanding. Then write a definition.

Rating Scale

1 I do not know this word.	2 I am not sure of the word's meaning.	3 I know this word. I can teach the word to someone else.

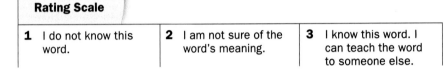

Key Word	Check Your Understanding	Deepen Your Understanding
1 attention (u-**ten**-shun) *noun* Rating: 1 2 3	☐ being noticed ☐ being ignored	My definition: _____ _____ _____ _____
2 device (di-**vīs**) *noun* Rating: 1 2 3	☐ a tool or machine ☐ an idea	My definition: _____ _____ _____ _____
3 disability (dis-u-**bi**-lu-tē) *noun* Rating: 1 2 3	☐ a condition that stops you from doing something ☐ a condition that stops you from remembering something	My definition: _____ _____ _____ _____
4 disadvantage (dis-ud-**van**-tij) *noun* Rating: 1 2 3	☐ something that makes life easier ☐ something that makes life more difficult	My definition: _____ _____ _____ _____

These friends are **social**. They **identify** with each other because they all like ice cream. ▶

Key Word	Check Your Understanding	Deepen Your Understanding
5 identify (ī-**den**-tu-fī) *verb* Rating: 1 2 3	☐ to write a story ☐ to connect with a group or an idea	My definition: _____ _____ _____ _____
6 separate (**se**-pu-rāt) *verb* Rating: 1 2 3	☐ to keep apart ☐ to keep together	My definition: _____ _____ _____ _____
7 situation (si-chu-**wā**-shun) *noun* Rating: 1 2 3	☐ a set of problems and ideas ☐ a set of events or circumstances	My definition: _____ _____ _____ _____
8 social (**sō**-shul) *adjective* Rating: 1 2 3	☐ alone ☐ with other people	My definition: _____ _____ _____ _____

Before Reading Cochlear Implants: Two Sides of the Story

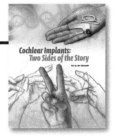

READING STRATEGY: Make Connections

How to MAKE CONNECTIONS

1. As you read, ask, "What do the writer's ideas and experiences remind me of? Do they remind me of something I experienced or heard about?"

2. Compare the writer's opinion with your own experience. Write your connections on self-stick notes.

3. When you are done reading, use your connections to help you decide whether you agree with the writer.

A. Read the text. Underline the writer's opinion. Then connect the writer's ideas to your own experiences. Write your connections on the self-stick notes.

Look Into the Text

I am a girl who happens to be deaf. I don't have a cochlear implant (CI). I don't plan to get one, ever. I feel that deaf people don't need to be able to hear to be happy.

I have a lot of friends who have a CI. Many of them think being able to hear is better than being deaf. Some people don't realize that CIs don't help you hear much.

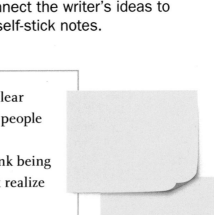

B. Do you agree with the writer? Use your connections to support your opinion. Share your work with a partner.

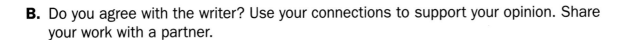

_____

_____

Selection Review Cochlear Implants: Two Sides of the Story

 How Important Is It to Fit In?
Learn what makes people feel good about themselves.

In "Cochlear Implants," you read about two deaf teens who have different ideas about fitting in.

A. Fill in the chart. Make connections to your own experiences. Then write whether you agree with the writer's opinion. Support your opinion.

Connections Chart

The text says . . .	My connection . . .	Agree or disagree?
"Instead of separating ourselves into little groups, we need to learn to respect our differences. Deep down we're all the same. I think we need to remember we have something in common. We're all part of one community."		
"If parents do want to put a CI on their child, they should wait until s/he is older. That way, the kid can decide what s/he really wants to do."		
"If you grew up in a family like mine, you would understand why I think it is such a great gift to be deaf. I don't think that there are enough people who prize their deafness."		

B. Use the connections you made to answer the questions.

1. What happens when people separate into groups?

_____

_____

2. What other kinds of gifts do you know of that are like Tanya's deafness?

_____

_____

Before Reading High School

READING STRATEGY: Make Connections

HOW TO MAKE CONNECTIONS

1. Read the text. Look for words that explain how the writer thinks or feels.

2. Ask, "Have I ever thought or felt this way?"

3. Decide how your connection improves your understanding of the text.

A. Read the text. Think about how the writer feels.

Look Into the Text

> Our generation fears someone knowing who you really are. Everybody is a faker. Everybody fronts. They act like they are somebody different.

B. Now make your own connection. Answer the questions.

1. Which words help you understand how the writer feels?

_____

_____

_____

2. Have you ever felt or thought this way?

I felt this way when _____

_____

_____

3. How does your connection help you understand the text?

_____

_____

_____

Connect Across Texts

In "Cochlear Implants," Caitlin and Tanya have different ideas about what it means to fit in. Find out what the high school students in this photo essay say about fitting in.

High School

by Jona Frank

Interact with the Text

1. Make Connections
Circle words that describe how people feel about being themselves. Do you know anyone who is afraid to tell the truth about himself or herself?

Our **generation** fears someone knowing who you really are. Everybody is **a faker**. Everybody **fronts**. They act like they are somebody different. When somebody finds out who they really are, that's when they get scared.

—New Jersey high school student

In Other Words
generation age group
a faker different from how they act (slang)
fronts pretends to be someone he or she is not (slang)

2. Make Connections

Lydia thinks that some people "climb the social ladder." Do you ever think or feel this way about someone?

_____

_____

_____

3. Make Connections

Do you understand the way Roberto feels? Why or why not? Explain your answer.

I do/don't understand

how Roberto feels because

_____

_____

_____

.

Fitting in is having a lot of people who are okay with who you are. You just want to belong to something. Then people start to **identify** you with it.

It's all one big **social** party. You see people try to **climb the social ladder**. You try to hang out with people to get higher socially.

—Lydia

I will be honest. I think we rule the school. We're not scared of anyone. No one can tell us what to do.

You are either **a jock**, a **bookworm**, or **an alternative person**. You make friends quickest by joining sports. When you are in the newspaper, you feel famous. People come up to you from other schools—people you don't know. They are like, "Great game." It's awesome.

—Roberto

Key Vocabulary
identify *verb*, to connect with a group or idea
social *adjective*, with other people

In Other Words
climb the social ladder make friends with the popular kids
a jock an athlete
bookworm person who reads and studies a lot
an alternative person a person who dresses and acts in a different way

The club started when I found out anything could be a club. I thought, why not have a club where you could have a lot of fun with no **structure**? Why not call it the Chris Blair Club? Now it's the second biggest club in the school, right behind the Debate Club. We once had sixty-five people at a meeting.

I love the **attention**. I'm just bored without the attention. If I'm not getting attention, I make something happen to get attention.

If I was wearing what you would consider all normal clothes, people wouldn't pay attention. If I'm wearing all black or makeup or the top hat, then people don't say anything to me, but they look. I get their eyes.

— Chris ❖

Key Vocabulary
attention *noun*, being noticed

In Other Words
structure rules

4. Make Connections
What is important to Chris? Circle the word he repeats. In your own words, explain how he feels.

_____

_____

_____

_____

5. Make Connections
Do you know someone who dresses in an unusual way, like Chris, to get attention? Explain.

_____

_____

_____

_____

Selection Review High School

A. Explain what each student thinks. Then make connections.

Connections Chart

The text says . . .	My connection . . .
The New Jersey high school student thinks everyone is afraid to be real. (page 179)	Some of my friends have this fear. They think that if they show who they are, people won't like them.
Lydia thinks _____ _____ . (page 180)	_____ _____
Roberto thinks _____ _____ . (page 180)	_____ _____
Chris thinks that _____ _____ . (page 181)	_____ _____

B. Now think about the connections you made to the students in the text and answer the questions.

1. Who did you connect with the most? Why?

_____

_____

2. How did your connection help you better understand the student's opinions?

_____

_____

Reflect and Assess

WRITING: Write About Literature

A. Plan your writing. Reread Roberto's statement from "High School." Use the chart to make notes and organize your thoughts. Tell if you agree or disagree with Roberto's statement by stating your opinion. Then list two reasons to support your opinion.

> "You are either a jock, a bookworm, or an alternative person."
>
> –Roberto

1. State Opinion	2. Support Opinion
I agree/disagree with Roberto's statement because I think _____	I think this because 1. _____ 2. _____

B. Write a paragraph to express your opinion. Use your notes.

_____

_____

_____

_____

_____

_____

_____

VOCABULARY STUDY: Use Context Clues for Multiple-Meaning Words

Some words are spelled the same but have more than one meaning. If you are not sure which meaning fits, try looking at the context. Pick the meaning that makes sense in the sentence.

> **play** (plā) *verb* **1** : to be active in a game **2** : to make music on an instrument

Many deaf students <u>play</u> sports.

> *The word "play" is used in a sports context. Sports are games. Here, "play" must mean "to be active in a game."*

A. Circle the context clue that helped you find the meaning of each underlined word.

1. Caitlin is deaf, but she <u>plays</u> the piano and the flute.

2. Students meet in the gym to <u>play</u> basketball.

B. Read the meanings of *poor* and *hearing*. After each sentence, circle number **1** or **2** to show the right meaning in that context.

> **poor** (pȯr) *adjective* **1** : without much money **2** : deserving someone's sympathy or help
>
> **hearing** (hir-ing) *noun* **1** : the ability to receive sounds **2** : the chance to explain something

3. Never think, "<u>Poor</u> me—I'm deaf."

  1 **2**

4. Cochlear implants cost money. Can <u>poor</u> people afford them?

  1 **2**

5. If you don't have your <u>hearing</u>, you live in a quiet world.

  1 **2**

6. I went to the public <u>hearing</u> about deafness. Now I understand cochlear implants better.

  1 **2**

COMPREHENSION: Distinguish Fact and Opinion

Facts are statements that can be proved as true.
Opinions are statements that tell what people think, feel, or believe.

To distinguish fact from opinion, follow these steps.

1. Read a statement. Ask, "Can this be proved as true or false?"

- If the answer is yes, then the statement is a fact.
- If the answer is no, then the statement is an opinion.

2. Look for words like *think* and *feel*. These words usually signal opinions.

Reread "Cochlear Implants." As you read Caitlin's speech and Tanya's letter, write statements in the Fact-and-Opinion Chart. Find at least two factual statements and two opinion statements from each selection.

Fact-and-Opinion Chart

Fact	Opinion
"I don't have a cochlear implant."	"I feel that deaf people don't need to be able to hear to be happy."

Prepare to Read

▶ **The Right Moves**
▶ **I'm Nobody**

Key Vocabulary

Circle a number to rate how well you know each word. Circle the word
that completes the sentence to check your understanding. Then
complete the sentences.

Rating Scale

1 I do not know this word.	**2** I am not sure of the word's meaning.	**3** I know this word. I can teach the word to someone else.

Key Word	Check Your Understanding	Deepen Your Understanding
❶ nervous (**nur**-vus) *adjective* Rating: 1 2 3	To be **nervous** is to be _____. **calm** **afraid**	When my dog is nervous, he _____ _____ _____ _____.
❷ nobody (**nō**-bu-dē) *pronoun;* *noun* Rating: 1 2 3	If you feel like a **nobody**, you do not feel _____. **important** **tall**	A person who is a nobody might feel _____ _____ _____ _____.
❸ participate (par-**ti**-su-pāt) *verb* Rating: 1 2 3	When you **participate**, you _____ an activity. **stay away from** **join in**	Many people participate in _____ _____ _____ _____.
❹ perform (pur-**form**) *verb* Rating: 1 2 3	To **perform** is to _____ a talent in front of people. **show** **hide**	At the talent show, Zak will perform _____ _____ _____ _____.

This girl is **somebody**. How do her classmates show their **support** for her? ▶

Key Word	Check Your Understanding	Deepen Your Understanding
⑤ somebody (**sum**-bu-dē) *pronoun; noun* Rating: 1 2 3	A **somebody** is a person who other people think is _____ . **important** **unimportant**	An example of a somebody is _____ _____ _____ _____ .
⑥ sponsor (**spon**-sur) *verb* Rating: 1 2 3	A **sponsor** is _____ for an activity. **responsible** **angry**	The supermarket will sponsor _____ _____ _____ _____ .
⑦ support (su-**port**) *noun* Rating: 1 2 3	If you offer **support**, you show that you _____ . **read** **care**	You can show support for our animal shelter by _____ _____ _____ _____ .
⑧ tension (**ten**-shun) *noun* Rating: 1 2 3	**Tension** is a feeling of worry and _____ . **energy** **stress**	Many people feel tension when they _____ _____ _____ _____ .

Before Reading The Right Moves

READING STRATEGY: Make Connections

HOW TO MAKE CONNECTIONS

1. As you read, stop occasionally and think about how the story connects to something in the world.

2. Ask, "Does the connection help me understand the events?" If so, write it in a **Connections Chart**.

3. Explain how it helps you better understand the text you are reading.

A. Read the text and look at the chart.

Look Into the Text

> Girls in our school wore trendy, brand-name clothes, but Lola sewed hers. Most kids talked about TV shows and movies, but Lola didn't even have a TV. She stood out like a sore thumb.

B. Read the text in the first column of the Connections Chart. Then write your connection to the text. In the last column, write how your connection helps you better understand the text.

Connections Chart

The text says . . .	My connection . . .	This helps me because . . .
"Girls in our school wore trendy, brand-name clothes, but Lola sewed hers."		

Selection Review The Right Moves

 How Important Is It to Fit In?
Talk about how people can create their own space.

In "The Right Moves," you read about someone who would rather be herself than fit in.

A. Reread "The Right Moves." Fill in the chart. Write how each part of the story connects to something in the world. Then write how the connection helps you better understand the text.

Connections Chart

The text says . . .	My connection . . .	This helps me because . . .
"I didn't want to stand out from the rest of the group, so I worked day and night to learn all the right moves."		
"'You're a great person and a wonderful dancer. Just be yourself.'"		
"For once, Lola didn't look like she was ignoring their comments. She looked scared."		
"Behind me, Maya gasped, but Lola saw me and smiled. Together, we faced the audience and sang our favorite song."		

B. Use the connections you made to answer the questions.

1. What did Lena learn from what happened at the talent show? _____

_____

2. What connection helped you understand why Lena says she is done trying to find all the right moves? _____

_____

Before Reading I'm Nobody

Compare Genres

HOW TO COMPARE GENRES

1. Look at how the text is organized.

2. Decide what kind of text you are reading.

3. Ask, "What does the author want me to understand from this text?"

A. Read the texts. Think about how they are organized differently. Complete the sentences.

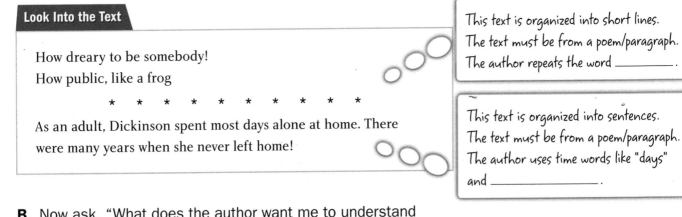

Look Into the Text

How dreary to be somebody!
How public, like a frog

*   *   *   *   *   *   *   *   *   *

As an adult, Dickinson spent most days alone at home. There were many years when she never left home!

This text is organized into short lines. The text must be from a poem/paragraph. The author repeats the word _____.

This text is organized into sentences. The text must be from a poem/paragraph. The author uses time words like "days" and _____.

B. Now ask, "What does the author want me to understand from this text?" Write your ideas.

In the first excerpt, the speaker wants me to understand that she _____

_____

_____.

In the second excerpt, the author wants me to understand that _____

_____

_____.

Connect Across Texts

In "The Right Moves," Lena gets attention when she **performs**. How does the speaker in this poem feel about getting attention?

I'm Nobody

by Emily Dickinson
Art by Sara Beazley

I'm nobody! Who are you?

Are you nobody, too?

Then there's a pair of us—don't tell!

They'd banish us, you know.

5 How dreary to be somebody!

How public, like a frog

To tell your name the livelong day

To an admiring bog!

Interact with the Text

1. Compare Genres

How is the text organized?

_____

_____

What kind of text are you reading?

_____

2. Make Connections

The poet says being famous is boring. Think about how the poet's idea connects to something in the world. How does your connection help you understand the text?

_____

_____

_____

_____

Key Vocabulary

perform *verb*, to show a talent to a group of people

nobody *noun*, a person who others think is not important

somebody *noun*, a person who others think is important

In Other Words

banish us make us go away

dreary boring

tell your name the livelong day talk about the same things all the time

an admiring bog a group of people who only pretend to admire you

Emily Dickinson

(1830–1886)

Interact with the Text

3. Compare Genres
How is this text different from the text on page 191?

4. Compare Genres
What does the author of this paragraph want you to understand?

The poet Emily Dickinson knew a lot about fitting in. Dickinson was a social person when she was young. When she left school, however, she became much **shier**. As an adult, Dickinson spent most days alone at home. There were many years when she never left home!

Emily Dickinson at about age 16.

In Other Words
shier more shy

Dickinson spent much of her time writing poetry. She wrote about nature, love, and death. She wrote more than one thousand poems. But Dickinson published fewer than ten poems when she was alive. Many of her **most famous** poems were **discovered** after her death.

Dickinson often wrote about being lonely. She did not have many **visitors**. But Dickinson was not all alone. She spent time at her home with a few close friends and family members. She also wrote many letters to friends. ❖

Dickinson probably wrote many of her poems in her quiet, plain bedroom.

Interact with the Text

5. Compare Genres

Underline the words the author uses to tell what kind of life Dickinson led. Circle the words that tell what the poet wrote about.

What does the author want you to understand about Dickinson's poems?

_____

_____

_____

_____

Dickinson lived in this house almost her entire life. Her brother and his family lived next door.

In Other Words
most famous best known
discovered found
visitors people who came to her house
  to see her

Selection Review I'm Nobody

A. Read the chart and write how the text is organized. Then decide what type of text you are reading.

Text	How Text Is Organized	Type of Text
"How dreary to be somebody! How public, like a frog To tell your name the livelong day To an admiring bog!"		
"Dickinson often wrote about being lonely. She did not have many visitors. But Dickinson was not all alone. She spent time at her home with a few close friends and family members…"		

B. Reread "I'm Nobody" and the biography of Emily Dickinson. What do you understand about Emily Dickinson from the texts?

_____

_____

_____

_____

Reflect and Assess

WRITING: Write About Literature

A. Plan your writing. List your talents in the chart. Then, mark an *X* to say whether you would perform the talent in a talent show at your school.

My Talents	Perform	Not Perform
Singing	X	

B. Choose one of your talents to write about. Read the student model.

Student Model

> If someone asked me to perform, I would say
> yes because I am a good singer and I like to
> sing in front of people.

C. Now write a paragraph to explain whether you would perform your talent. Include at least two reasons to explain your decision.

_____

_____

_____

_____

_____

_____

_____

Integrate the Language Arts

VOCABULARY STUDY: Use Example Clues

Examples can give clues to a word's meaning. To figure out the meaning of an unknown word:

- Look for an example in a sentence nearby.
- Think about how the example makes the text clear.

> **Example:** Marc painted <u>foreign</u> scenes. For example, he painted landscapes in Kenya and a marketplace in China.

Kenya and China are examples of other countries. "Foreign" must mean "from other countries."

A. Circle the words that help you learn the meaning of the underlined word.

1. Marc was not <u>wealthy</u>. He had little money for art supplies.

2. He wanted to be a <u>renowned</u> artist, like Leonardo da Vinci or Pablo Picasso. Everyone knows them.

3. Marc <u>devoted</u> himself to his goal. He practiced every day, drawing on every piece of paper he could find.

B. Think about the underlined words. Use example clues to figure out the meanings. Then write what you think each word means.

4. Would Marc ever be a <u>popular</u> artist? Would lots of people like his artwork someday?

_____

5. He wanted people to <u>respect</u> him. Maybe they could say, "Good work." Maybe they could cheer. Maybe they even could buy his paintings.

_____

6. His teacher said, "You have real <u>drive</u>, Marc. For example, you try hard to make your paintings great. No other art student works harder than you do!"

_____

© NGSP & HB

LITERARY ANALYSIS: Compare Characters

Authors sometimes create characters that are very different. These differences can help you understand the story. Compare the characters in "The Right Moves."

A. Fill in the chart. Write what each character does. Then write what each character's actions show about her. Write how the characters are the same and how they are different.

Character Description Chart

Character	What the Character Does	What This Shows About the Character	Summary Comparison
Lola	She sews her own clothes.	She is not afraid to be different.	Similarities: _____ _____ _____
Lena	_____ _____ _____	_____ _____ _____	Differences: _____ _____ _____

B. Write a summary that compares Lola and Lena. Tell how the comparison helps you understand the story. Use your notes.

_____

_____

_____

_____

_____

_____

_____

Vocabulary Review

A. Study each picture. Circle the word that completes each sentence.

1.

Friends should **(arrive / support)** each other.

2.

He gets **(attention / situation)** when he dances.

3.

Being unable to walk is a **(disability / agreement)**.

4.

It is a **(somebody / disadvantage)** to write with a cast on your arm.

B. Choose words to complete the webs below.

arrive	belong	nervous	prepare	sponsor
believe	jealous	perform	social	suggest

Word Web

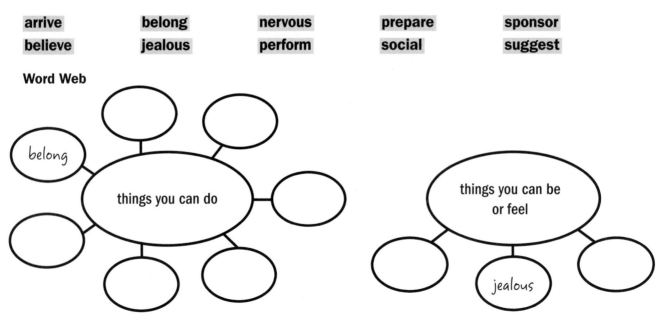

belong

things you can do

things you can be or feel

jealous

Unit 5 Vocabulary

agreement	belong	identify	ordinary	situation	support
alone	device	jealous	participate	social	tension
arrive	disability	judgment	perform	somebody	
attention	disadvantage	nervous	prepare	sponsor	
believe	exotic	nobody	separate	suggest	

C. Choose words to complete the sentences below.

alone	exotic	ordinary	separate
device	identify	participate	tension

1. Teresa hoped someone would visit. She did not like being _____ .

2. I can _____ with anyone who likes football.

3. Some students wore fancy clothes at the dance, but Kyle wore jeans and an _____ white shirt.

4. _____ the beads into these boxes. Put the round ones here and the square ones there.

5. That strange, _____ music makes me want to dance!

6. When I finished taking the test, my _____ went away.

7. The race is next Saturday. Will you _____ in it?

8. A flashlight is a good _____ to have at night.

Unit Vocabulary

Circle a number to rate how well you know each word. Circle the word that completes the sentence to check your understanding. Then write a definition.

▲ Angie has a good **attitude**. She will have **success** solving the problem.

Rating Scale		
1 I do not know this word.	**2** I am not sure of the word's meaning.	**3** I know this word. I can teach the word to someone else.

Key Word	Check Your Understanding	Deepen Your Understanding
1 success (suk-**ses**) *noun* Rating: **1 2 3**	**Success** is when you reach your _____. **goal** **shelf**	 My definition: _____ _____ _____
2 wealth (**welth**) *noun* Rating: **1 2 3**	If you have **wealth**, you have _____ of something. **a lot** **very little**	 My definition: _____ _____ _____
3 attitude (**a**-tu-tüd) *noun* Rating: **1 2 3**	A _____ person has a good **attitude**. **positive** **tall**	 My definition: _____ _____ _____

Vocabulary Workshop

Interpret Figurative Language

The exact meaning of a word is the **literal** meaning. **Figurative language** goes beyond the literal meaning.

Use different strategies to interpret figurative language.

- Use context clues. Look for words that suggest a comparison.
- Form a mental picture from the language. Decide what feeling or image the writer is trying to create.

Practice Interpreting Figurative Language

Read the passage. Identify each underlined phrase. Circle *idiom* or *simile*. Then write the meaning.

A Surprise for Sara

We are going to have a party for Sara's birthday. The party is a surprise, though, so do not spill the beans. I will be as angry as a bull if Sara finds out!

KINDS OF FIGURATIVE LANGUAGE
An **idiom** is a group of words that does not match the literal meaning of its words.
A **simile** uses words such as *like, as,* and *than* to compare two unlike things.

1. spill the beans   (idiom / simile)   Meaning: _____

2. as angry as a bull   (idiom / simile)   Meaning: _____

Put the Strategy to Use

Write the meaning of each underlined phrase.

3. School is important to me. I hit the books every day. _____

4. But I like to have fun, too. My friend Sara says I am the life of the party.

_____

5. In some ways, Sara and I are as different as night and day. _____

6. Like me, Sara cares about people. She has a heart of gold. _____

Prepare to Read

▶ Luck
▶ Young at Heart

Key Vocabulary

Circle a number to rate how well you know each word. Circle *yes* or *no* to check your understanding. Then write a definition.

Rating Scale		
1 I do not know this word.	**2** I am not sure of the word's meaning.	**3** I know this word. I can teach the word to someone else.

Key Word	Check Your Understanding	Deepen Your Understanding
1 exchange (iks-**chānj**) *verb* Rating: 1 2 3	I **exchange** a shirt when it does not fit me. **Yes** **No**	My definition: _____ _____ _____ _____
2 fair (**fār**) *adjective* Rating: 1 2 3	It is **fair** to invite only the popular kids to a party. **Yes** **No**	My definition: _____ _____ _____ _____
3 inspire (in-**spīr**) *verb* Rating: 1 2 3	Stories about heroes do not **inspire** people. **Yes** **No**	My definition: _____ _____ _____ _____
4 luck (**luk**) *noun* Rating: 1 2 3	It is good **luck** to miss the bus. **Yes** **No**	My definition: _____ _____ _____ _____

She makes an **offer** to buy the basket. The seller will **exchange** the basket for money. ▶

Key Word	Check Your Understanding	Deepen Your Understanding
5 offer (**ah**-fur) *noun* Rating: 1 2 3	She will make an **offer** to buy her father's car. Yes No	My definition: _____ _____ _____ _____
6 refuse (ri-**fyüz**) *verb* Rating: 1 2 3	I enjoyed that movie. I **refuse** to see it again. Yes No	My definition: _____ _____ _____ _____
7 reveal (ri-**vēl**) *verb* Rating: 1 2 3	He put his hat on. He did not want to **reveal** his hair. Yes No	My definition: _____ _____ _____ _____
8 spirit (**spir**-ut) *noun* Rating: 1 2 3	That happy man has a joyful **spirit**. Yes No	My definition: _____ _____ _____ _____

Before Reading Luck

READING STRATEGY: Make Inferences

How to Make Inferences

1. As you read, look for clues and details the author gives you about the characters and events.

2. Use what you know about people to make sense of the story. Connect your own experience to the details.

3. Track your thoughts on an **Inference Chart** like the one below.

A. Read the text.

Look Into the Text

> **ACTOR 2.** Why don't we move to the mountain?
>
> **ACTOR 3.** Because there are only five houses there, and they took them all.
>
> **ACTOR 4.** Maybe we can exchange our houses for theirs.
>
> **ACTOR 5.** What a great idea!
>
> **ACTOR 3.** Naw. They probably won't want to do that.
>
> **ACTOR 4.** Maybe we should pay them some extra money.

B. Connect your own experience to the text. Use the Inference Chart.

Inference Chart

I read . . .	I know . . .	And so . . .
"Maybe we should pay them some extra money."	If you pay someone a lot of money,	

Selection Review Luck

 EQ **What Is Most Important in Life?**
Think about how your attitude affects your life.

A. In "Luck," you learned that your attitude might be more important than luck. Read the details in the Inference Chart. Then fill in the chart. Write inferences about those details.

Inference Chart

I read . . .	I know . . .	And so . . .
"We are interested in exchanging houses. Our houses are very nice."		
"I had no idea that life was so pleasant down here in the valley."		
"You said before that you liked living on the mountain."		
"The main thing is that we are so lucky to be here on the mountain."		

B. Make inferences to answer the questions.

1. How do the valley people feel after they move to the mountain? How do you know?

_____

_____

2. Will the valley people be happy when they move back to the valley? How do you know?

_____

_____

Before Reading Young at Heart

Genre: Memoir

HOW TO READ A MEMOIR

1. Read the text. Find important details about people and events. Write them on self-stick notes.

2. Ask, "Why did the author choose these details?"

3. Connect the details to the author's message. Think about what influenced his or her personality or beliefs.

A. Read the text. Write important details on the self-stick notes.

Look Into the Text

One of my grandmother's great passions was theater. This passion never diminished with age. She never missed a show when there were actors in town. If no actors came for several months, she would organize her own show. She was the manager, the producer, and the young heroine, all at the same time.

B. Think about the important details. Answer the questions.

1. What is the author trying to show about his grandmother?

_____

_____

2. How do you think the author's grandmother influenced him?

_____

_____

Connect Across Texts

In "Luck," the characters' view of what's important changes. In the following memoir, the writer tells about his grandmother's lifelong love of **theater**.

YOUNG AT HEART

BY HUYNH QUANG NHUONG

When she was eighty years old, my grandmother was still quite strong. Every two days, she walked for more than an hour to reach the marketplace. She carried **a heavy load** of food. Then she spent another hour walking home.

My grandmother was quite old. But **traces** of her beauty were still there. Her hands, her feet, her face **revealed** that she had been **an attractive** young woman. Time didn't damage her youthful **spirit**.

Key Vocabulary
reveal *verb*, to show or tell something that was hidden
spirit *noun*, the way you act, think, and feel

In Other Words
theater plays
a heavy load heavy bags
traces signs
an attractive a pretty

3. Memoir

Underline a detail that supports this sentence: "Time didn't damage her youthful spirit."

How do you think this detail supports the author's message?

_____

_____

_____

_____

_____

_____

_____

4. Make Inferences

What does the author mean when he says that the grandmother's plays were inspired by the books she read and the plays she saw?

_____

_____

_____

_____

_____

_____

_____

One of my grandmother's great **passions** was theater. This passion **never diminished** with age. She never missed a show when there were actors in town. If no actors came for several months, she would **organize** her own show. She was the manager, the producer, and the young **heroine**, all at the same time.

My grandmother's own plays were always dramas. They were **inspired** by books she had read and by what she had seen on the stage. She always chose her favorite grandson to play the role of the hero. He would always marry the heroine at the end. And they lived happily **ever after**.

Key Vocabulary
inspire *verb*, to make someone want to do something

In Other Words
passions loves
never diminished did not get less powerful
organize create
heroine female actor with the most important role
ever after for the rest of their lives

My sisters told her that she was too old to play the young heroine. But my grandmother merely replied: "Anybody can play this role if she's young at heart." ❖

5. Make Inferences

Think about what the sisters told the grandmother. What does this detail tell you?

_____

_____

_____

_____

6. Memoir

Underline the words that the grandmother says. Why do you think the author includes this detail?

_____

_____

_____

_____

_____

Selection Review Young at Heart

A. Write details about the author's grandmother in "Young at Heart." Complete the web.

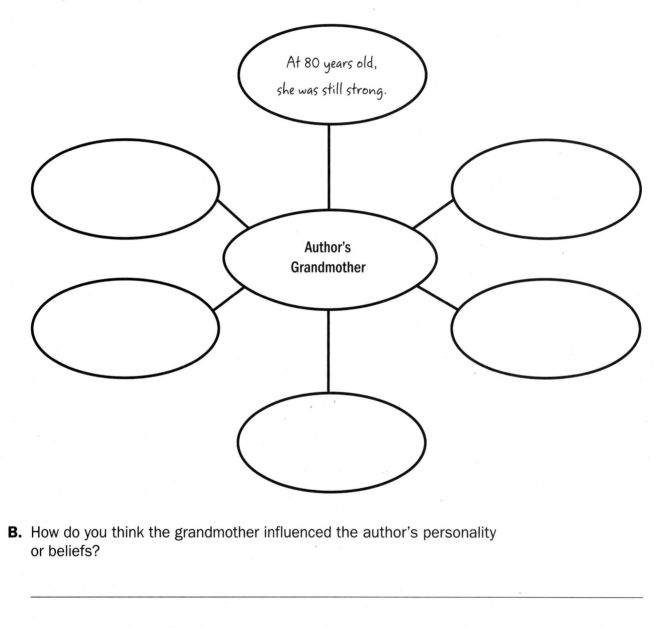

At 80 years old, she was still strong.

Author's Grandmother

B. How do you think the grandmother influenced the author's personality or beliefs?

_____

_____

_____

_____

Reflect and Assess

WRITING: Write About Literature

A. What makes people happy? What makes you happy? Plan your writing.
Review the selections. Then complete the chart.

"Luck"	"Young at Heart"	My Life	Topic Statement
The people from the mountain are happy when _____ _____ _____ _____ _____ _____ _____ .	The grandmother is happy when _____ _____ _____ _____ _____ _____ _____ .	I am happy when _____ _____ _____ _____ _____ _____ _____ .	People are happy with their lives when _____ _____ _____ _____ _____ _____ _____ .

B. Write a paragraph that explains what makes people happy. Begin with your
topic statement. Then support your opinion with examples from the selections
and from your own life. Use the chart to help you.

_____

_____

_____

_____

_____

_____

_____

VOCABULARY STUDY: Review Similes

A simile is one kind of figurative language. Similes use words such as *like*, *as*, and *than* to compare two unlike things. Writers use similes to create certain feelings or images in readers' minds.

> The leader of the valley people was as clever as a fox.

> The leader is being compared to a fox. Foxes are clever, or smart, animals. The leader must be smart, too.

A. Read each sentence. Name the two things that the simile compares.

1. Our leader was as tough as nails, but he spoke well.

_____ is being compared to _____ .

2. In a voice like silk, he talked about the houses on the mountain.

_____ is being compared to _____ .

3. We were more eager than kids in a candy store.

_____ are being compared to _____ .

4. Like lightning, we raced up the mountain.

_____ are being compared to _____ .

B. Read each simile. Then write what you think the sentence means.

5. We bought the houses on the mountain. At first, I felt as happy as a cat in a fish store.

_____

6. The mountain weather was hard, though. I was colder than an icicle!

_____

7. It was hard to walk around there, too. Even a short walk was like running a marathon.

_____

8. One fact was as clear as crystal: We needed our old homes back!

_____

LITERARY ANALYSIS: Literary Element: Setting

The setting of a story is when and where it takes place. In many stories, the setting affects how characters act and feel. "Luck" has two different settings.

A. Review "Luck." Look for words and phrases that describe the setting. Write them in the first column of the Setting Chart.

Setting Chart

Setting	How the Characters Feel About the Setting
Valley: – in the shadows – warmer	The valley people _____ _____ _____ . The mountain people _____ _____ _____ _____ _____ _____ .
Mountain:	The valley people _____ _____ . The mountain people _____ _____ _____ _____ .

B. Analyze the words and phrases in the first column of your chart. Then read the following questions. Write your answers in the second column of the chart. Discuss the questions in a group.

1. How do the characters who first live in the valley (the valley people) feel about where they live? How do the characters who first live on the mountain (the mountain people) feel about where they live?

2. After they move, how do the valley people feel about the setting? How do the mountain people feel about the setting?

Prepare to Read

▶ The Scholarship Jacket
▶ Eye on Cheaters

Key Vocabulary

Circle a number to rate how well you know each word. Mark an *X* next to the correct definition to check your understanding. Then complete the sentences.

Rating Scale		
1 I do not know this word.	**2** I am not sure of the word's meaning.	**3** I know this word. I can teach the word to someone else.

Key Word	Check Your Understanding	Deepen Your Understanding
❶ behavior (bi-**hā**-vyur) *noun* **Rating: 1 2 3**	☐ the way you act ☐ the way you think	An example of polite **behavior** is _____ _____ _____ _____.
❷ cheat (**chēt**) *verb* **Rating: 1 2 3**	☐ to be fair and follow the rules ☐ to do something unfair or against the rules	A student might **cheat** by _____ _____ _____ _____
❸ dignity (**dig**-nu-tē) *noun* **Rating: 1 2 3**	☐ tension ☐ self-respect	Most people act with **dignity** when they go to _____ _____ _____ _____
❹ honest (**ah**-nust) *adjective* **Rating: 1 2 3**	☐ truthful ☐ jealous	The reporter was not **honest**. He _____ _____ _____ _____

I **recognize** this graduation **tradition**! ▶

Key Word	Check Your Understanding	Deepen Your Understanding
5 **integrity** (in-**te**-gru-tē) *noun* Rating: 1 2 3	☐ when you do what you know is wrong ☐ when you do what you know is right	**Integrity** also could be called _____ _____ _____ _____.
6 **recognize** (**re**-kig-nīz) *verb* Rating: 1 2 3	☐ to know people or places ☐ to forget people or places	You will **recognize** my brother easily because he _____ _____ _____ _____.
7 **standard** (**stan**-durd) *noun* Rating: 1 2 3	☐ a level of sadness ☐ a level of goodness	Someone who has a high **standard** always _____ _____ _____ _____.
8 **tradition** (tru-**di**-shun) *noun* Rating: 1 2 3	☐ a way of doing things ☐ doing things differently every time	One **tradition** of Thanksgiving is _____ _____ _____ _____.

Before Reading The Scholarship Jacket

READING STRATEGY: Make Inferences

HOW TO MAKE INFERENCES

1. Read the story. Notice details about how a character acts. Write them in the first column of an **Inference Chart**.

2. Think about what you already know. In the second column of your chart, write what you know about how people act.

3. Combine what you know with what you read to make an inference about the character. Write it in the third column of your chart.

A. Read the text about the character Marta.

Look Into the Text

> Standing with all the dignity I could muster, I said, "I'll speak to my grandfather about it, sir, and let you know tomorrow." I cried on the walk home from the bus stop.

B. Now make an inference about Marta. What do you know about people who are in similar situations? Complete the chart.

Inference Chart

I read . . .	I know . . .	And so . . .
"Standing with all the dignity I could muster . . ."		

Selection Review The Scholarship Jacket

 What Is Most Important in Life?
Explore what it means to do the right thing.

A. In "The Scholarship Jacket," you learned that doing the right thing can sometimes be hard. Write what you already know about similar actions. Use your knowledge to make an inference about Marta. Complete the Inference Chart.

Inference Chart

I read . . .	I know . . .	And so . . .
"I looked him straight in the eye. He looked away."		
"I dragged myself into the principal's office the next day."		
"I sat very straight in my chair."		
"I wanted to yell, jump, run the mile, do something."		

B. Use your inferences to answer the questions.

1. The next day, Marta forces her eyes to stay dry while she talks with the principal. What does this say about her?

_____

_____

2. Why does Marta skip and whistle on her way back to the house?

_____

_____

Before Reading Eye on Cheaters

TEXT STRUCTURE: Cause and Effect

HOW TO IDENTIFY CAUSES AND EFFECTS

1. Read the text.

2. Identify something that happens. Ask, "What happened? and Why did it happen?" The reason why it happened is the cause. The result, or what happened, is the effect.

3. Record the information in a **Cause-and-Effect Chart**.

A. Read the text.

Look Into the Text

> Donald McCabe led the Rutgers University study about cheating. He says the Internet is partly to blame. "The Internet makes plagiarism very simple."
>
> McCabe also thinks that cheating and corruption by famous adults are to blame. "I think kids today are looking to adults . . . for a moral compass. When they see the behavior occurring there, they don't understand why they should be held to a higher standard," he explained.

B. Based on the text above, why do kids cheat? Write each reason in a Cause box.

Cause-and-Effect Chart

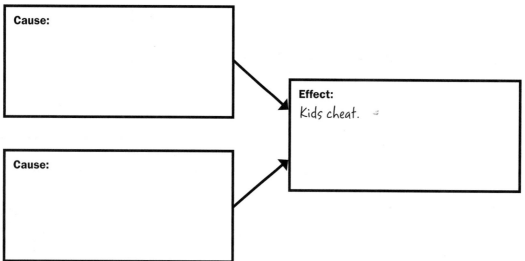

Cause:

Cause:

Effect:
Kids cheat.

Eye on Cheaters

from *CURRENT EVENTS*, JAN. 9, 2004

THIS IS A TEST. Clear off your desks, and get your pencils.

1. A friend steals a copy of your social studies test. You

   (A) **high-five** him.

   (B) tell your teacher. **Cheating** is wrong.

2. You studied for your exam. Still, you just can't remember all those vocabulary words. You

   (A) look at the paper of the smart girl who sits next to you.

   (B) answer the questions you know. Next time you'll study harder.

3. You are doing research for a book report. You find a Web site that has essays already written. They're pretty good. You

   (A) **hit copy, then paste!**

   (B) write your own paper. Your ideas are better anyway.

Key Vocabulary
integrity *noun*, doing what you know is right
cheat *verb*, to do something that is unfair or against the rules

In Other Words
high-five show that you are proud of
hit copy, then paste! use the essay from the Internet instead of writing your own.

Interact with the Text

1. Cause and Effect
Read each test question. Underline the things that cause students to cheat. Then complete the chart.

Causes:
- Students may study but may not _____
  _____
  _____ .

- It's easy to find _____
  _____
  _____ .

Effect:
Students copy others' work.

2. Cause and Effect

Underline the words that explain what has happened to cheating over time. Decide if this is a cause or an effect. Complete the chart.

```
┌─────────────────────┐
│ Cause:              │
│                     │
│                     │
│                     │
│                     │
│                     │
└─────────────────────┘
          │
          ▼
┌─────────────────────┐
│ Effect:             │
│                     │
│                     │
│                     │
│                     │
└─────────────────────┘
```

DID YOU ANSWER "A" to any of the questions? If so, you're one of a growing number of students who cheat. If you answered "B," chances are the person next to you tried to copy your answers.

In 2002, the Josephson Institute of Ethics surveyed twelve thousand high-school students. It found that 74 percent cheated at least once that year. That's up from 61 percent ten years before.

Why has the number of cheaters risen so much? Donald McCabe led the Rutgers University study about cheating. He says the Internet is partly to blame. "The Internet makes **plagiarism** very **simple**."

In Other Words

plagiarism copying the work of others
simple easy

Social Studies Background

Copyright laws protect ideas and words. Adults who plagiarize sometimes lose their jobs or have to pay money to the person they have stolen from.

McCabe also thinks that cheating and **corruption** by famous adults are to blame. "I think kids today are looking to adults . . . for **a moral compass**. When they see the behavior occurring there, they don't understand why they should be held to a higher standard," he explained.

What do cheaters have to say for themselves? Half of students asked said that they didn't think copying answers was wrong.

"I think cheating has become . . . 'normal' in some cases," wrote one student.

Another responded, "You do what it takes to **succeed** in life. We're afraid **to fail**."

High-school senior Alice Newhall said: "What's important is getting ahead. . . . If you learn to **cut corners** to do that, you're going to be saving yourself time and energy. In the real world, that's what's going on. The better you do, that's what shows. It's not how moral you were in getting there."

Key Vocabulary
behavior *noun*, the way a person acts
standard *noun*, a measure of how good something is

In Other Words
corruption lying and stealing
a moral compass an understanding of what is right and what is wrong
succeed get what you want
to fail we will not get what we want
cut corners use work that isn't yours

Interact with the Text

3. Cause and Effect
Underline other reasons for cheating. Add them to the chart.

Causes:
· Kids see _____

· Kids don't think that _____

·

·

Effect:
Kids cheat.

Interact with the Text

4. Cause and Effect

Underline the words that explain what happens at Marple Newtown High School. What do the committee members hope will happen as a result?

_____

_____

5. Make Inferences

Think about what you already know about how people behave. How can talking about cheating be useful?

_____

_____

_____

_____

_____

_____

TO FIGHT THE PROBLEM, some schools have a **secret weapon**—students. Marple Newtown High School in Philadelphia is one of a growing number of schools with student "academic integrity **committees**." At Marple, students on the committee visit classrooms to talk about cheating.

Committee leader Joey Borson, a senior, thinks the committee is useful. "Is there anything more important than your word? If you don't have your word or your honor, **what's the point**?"

In Other Words
secret weapon good solution
committees groups
what's the point? you have nothing.

THIS IS ANOTHER TEST. Take out your pencils and try again.

1. When you look at a friend's paper to get or check an answer, you
   - (A) lie about what you know.
   - (B) make it worse for yourself in the future. When questions get harder, you will not know the basics.

2. When you let a friend copy your work, you
   - (A) rob your friend of knowledge.
   - (B) make your own work **less valuable**.

3. When you copy something from a book or Web site, you
   - (A) **break the law** by stealing from someone.
   - (B) miss the chance to share information in your own voice.

ON THIS TEST, every answer shows the negative impact of cheating. What other ways does cheating **impact** you and others? ❖

In Other Words
less valuable worth less
break the law go against the law
impact affect

Interact with the Text

6. Cause and Effect
What are the effects of copying another person's work? Underline the words that explain.

7. Cause and Effect
What happens when you let a friend copy your work? Write the effects in the chart.

Cause:
You let a friend copy your work.

↓

Effects:
• You _____ _____ _____.
• You _____ _____ _____.

8. Make Inferences
How can letting a friend copy your work make the work less valuable?

_____
_____
_____

Selection Review Eye on Cheaters

A. According to the article, why are more students cheating? List some causes in the chart.

Cause-and-Effect Chart

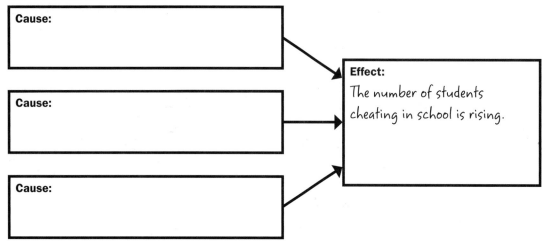

Cause:

Cause:

Cause:

Effect:
The number of students cheating in school is rising.

B. What are some effects of cheating? Add them to the chart below.

Cause-and-Effect Chart

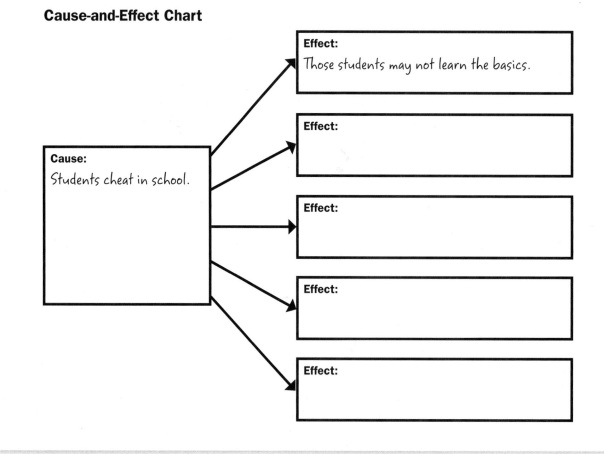

Cause:
Students cheat in school.

Effect:
Those students may not learn the basics.

Effect:

Effect:

Effect:

Effect:

WRITING: Write About Literature

A. When you "give your word," people trust you. Think about this quotation from "Eye on Cheaters": "Is there anything more important than your word?" What do you think is the answer? Use the chart to organize your ideas.

Opinion	Reasons
There is nothing more important than your word.	
Some things are more important than your word.	

B. Write a paragraph to explain your position. Give at least two reasons for your opinion. Use the chart to help you.

_____

_____

_____

_____

_____

_____

VOCABULARY STUDY: Review Idioms

Remember, an idiom is a kind of figurative language. Its meaning does not match the literal, or exact, meaning of its words. You can often use the context to figure out the meaning.

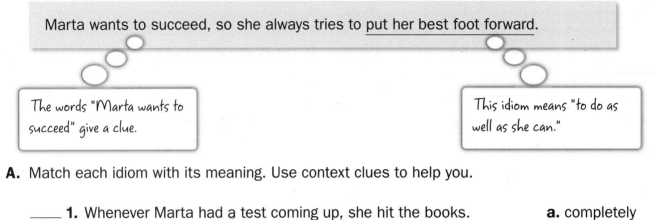

Marta wants to succeed, so she always tries to put her best foot forward.

The words "Marta wants to succeed" give a clue.

This idiom means "to do as well as she can."

A. Match each idiom with its meaning. Use context clues to help you.

_____ **1.** Whenever Marta had a test coming up, she hit the books.　　　**a.** completely

_____ **2.** She liked math tests. To her, they were a piece of cake.　　　**b.** studied hard

_____ **3.** She didn't always get an A. But she didn't get　　　**c.** very easy
bent out of shape if she got a B.

_____ **4.** Instead, she studied harder so she learned what she　　　**d.** upset
needed to know by heart.

B. Read each sentence. Use context clues to figure out the meaning of the idiom. Then write what you think the idiom means.

5. With a report card full of *A*'s, Marta was at the top of her class.

_____

6. The news about the jacket upset Marta. All day, she felt down in the dumps.

_____

7. Marta really stuck her neck out when she bravely declared that they would

not pay for the jacket.

_____

8. The principal backed down, and Marta got the jacket!

_____

LITERARY ANALYSIS: Literary Element: Plot

The plot is the sequence, or order, of action in a story. It begins with a **problem** and includes **events** that make the problem worse. The **turning point** is when the problem stops getting worse. It happens in the middle. The **solution** to the problem happens at the end.

A. Reread "The Scholarship Jacket." Then fill in the Plot Diagram with a partner.

Plot Diagram

② Middle

Turning Point: _____

_____

Event: _____

_____

Event: _____

_____

Event: _____

_____

③ End

Solution: _____

_____

_____

① Beginning

Problem: _____

_____

_____

B. Use the completed diagram to describe the plot of "The Scholarship Jacket." Then read your description to your partner.

_____

_____

_____

_____

_____

Prepare to Read

▷ **The Gift of the Magi**
▷ **Shoulders**

Key Vocabulary

Circle a number to rate how well you know each word. Circle the word that completes the sentence to check your understanding. Then write a definition.

Rating Scale		
1 I do not know this word.	**2** I am not sure of the word's meaning.	**3** I know this word. I can teach the word to someone else.

Key Word	Check Your Understanding	Deepen Your Understanding
❶ generosity (je-nu-**rah**-su-tē) *noun* Rating: 1 2 3	To show **generosity** is to _____ easily. **share** **sing**	My definition: _____ _____ _____ _____
❷ invent (in-**vent**) *verb* Rating: 1 2 3	When you **invent**, you make something _____. **old** **new**	My definition: _____ _____ _____ _____
❸ precious (**pre**-shus) *adjective* Rating: 1 2 3	When something is **precious**, it has great _____. **value** **damage**	My definition: _____ _____ _____ _____
❹ proud (**prowd**) *adjective* Rating: 1 2 3	To feel **proud** is to feel _____ about something you have done. **happy** **sad**	My definition: _____ _____ _____ _____

What might this **sensitive** child **wish** to have? ▶

Key Word	Check Your Understanding	Deepen Your Understanding
5 **reflect** (ri-**flekt**) *verb* Rating: **1** **2** **3**	To **reflect** is to show or _____ something. **watch** **represent**	My definition: _____ _____ _____ _____
6 **sacrifice** (**sa**-kru-fīs) *verb* Rating: **1** **2** **3**	When you **sacrifice** something, you _____ . **lose it** **keep it**	My definition: _____ _____ _____ _____
7 **sensitive** (**sen**-su-tiv) *adjective* Rating: **1** **2** **3**	A **sensitive** person is easily _____ . **hurt** **smart**	My definition: _____ _____ _____ _____
8 **wish** (**wish**) *verb* Rating: **1** **2** **3**	To **wish** for something is to _____ it very much. **hate** **want**	My definition: _____ _____ _____ _____

READING STRATEGY: Make Inferences

HOW TO MAKE INFERENCES

1. Preview the text. Look at the pictures. Notice details about them. Write details in the first column of an **Inference Chart**.

2. Think about what you already know about the subject of the picture. Write it in the second column of your chart.

3. Combine what you know with what you see to make an inference about the characters or events. Write your inference in the third column.

A. Look at the picture.

Look Into the Text

B. Now complete the Inference Chart.

Inference Chart

I see . . .	I know . . .	And so . . .

Selection Review   The Gift of the Magi

What Is Most Important in Life?
Consider how love matters.

A. In "The Gift of the Magi," Jim and Della show how much love matters. Look at each picture. Write what you see. Write what you know about the subject of the picture. Then write an inference about the characters or events.

Inference Chart

Picture	I see . . .	I know . . .	And so . . .

B. Look at the second picture. How does Della feel about her

gift? How do you know? _____

_____

Before Reading Shoulders

Elements of Poetry: Free Verse

> ### HOW TO READ FREE VERSE
>
> **1.** Read the poem.
>
> **2.** Identify words and phrases that form pictures in your mind.
>
> **3.** Think about how they affect you. Ask, "How do the pictures in my mind make me feel?"

A. Read the text from the poem. Underline words that form pictures in your mind.

Look Into the Text

> A man crosses the street in rain,
>
> stepping gently, looking two times north and south,
>
> because his son is asleep on his shoulder.

B. Write about the pictures that formed in your mind as you read.

_____

_____

_____

_____

_____

C. How do the pictures affect you? Describe your feelings to a partner.

Shoulders

BY NAOMI SHIHAB NYE

ILLUSTRATED BY MURRAY KIMBER

A man **crosses** the street in rain,
stepping **gently**, looking two times north and south,
because his son is asleep on his shoulder.

No car must **splash** him.
5 No car drive too near to his shadow.

Key Vocabulary
precious *adjective*, having great value

In Other Words
crosses walks to the other side of
gently carefully
splash get water on

Interact with the Text

1. Free Verse
Read lines 4–5. What picture forms in your mind? How does it make you feel? Complete the sentences.

In my mind, I see

_____

_____ .

The picture makes me feel

_____ .

2. Make Inferences
What kind of person is the man? Make an inference about him based on his actions and on the drawing.

_____

_____

_____

_____

3. Free Verse

Read lines 6–9. Circle words and phrases that might make you feel nervous.

4. Free Verse

Read lines 10–12. How do they make you feel? Why? Complete the sentence.

These lines make me feel

_____

because _____

_____

_____

_____ .

This man carries the world's most sensitive cargo

but **he's not marked**.

Nowhere does his jacket say FRAGILE,

HANDLE WITH CARE.

10　His ear fills up with breathing.

He hears the hum of a boy's dream

deep inside him.

Key Vocabulary

sensitive *adjective*, easily affected, changed, or hurt

In Other Words

he's not marked he doesn't come with instructions

We're not going to be able
to live in this world

15   if we're not willing to do what he's doing
with one another.

The road will only be wide.
The rain will never stop falling.

Interact with the Text

5. Free Verse
What picture do the poet's words form in your mind?

When I read these words,

I picture _____

_____

_____

6. Make Inferences
Why will people *not* be able to live in this world unless they act as the man acts? Use the image to help you make an inference.

_____

_____

_____

About the Poet

Naomi Shihab Nye (1952–) is a poet, songwriter, and author of children's books. She likes to write about the beautiful details in life. "We think in poetry. But some people pretend poetry is far away."

Selection Review Shoulders

A. Read the sentences from the poem. Describe the pictures they create in your mind. Then describe how they make you feel. Complete the chart.

Line	Picture in My Mind	Feeling
"No car drive too near to his shadow." (line 5)		
"His ear fills up with breathing." (line 10)		
"The rain will never stop falling." (line 18)		

B. Use your chart to explain the message of the poem. What is the poet trying to tell us?

_____

_____

Reflect and Assess

WRITING: Write About Literature

A. Plan your writing. Jim and Della sacrificed precious things to buy gifts for each other. What did they sacrifice? Why were those things so precious?

_____

_____

_____

_____

B. Think about the people you love. Then think about the things in your life that are precious to you. Make a list.

_____

C. What important thing would you be willing to give up for the people you love? Explain why. Write about this question for two minutes.

_____

_____

_____

_____

_____

_____

_____

_____

VOCABULARY STUDY: Review Idioms

Remember, an idiom is a kind of figurative language. Its meaning does not match the literal, or exact, meaning of its words. You can often use context to figure out the meaning.

The weather is so stormy today! It is <u>raining cats and dogs</u>.

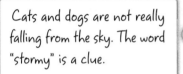

Cats and dogs are not really falling from the sky. The word "stormy" is a clue.

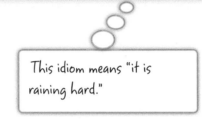

This idiom means "it is raining hard."

A. Match each idiom with its meaning. Use context clues to help you.

____ **1.** The father <u>keeps an eye out</u> for cars as he crosses the street.

____ **2.** He doesn't <u>drag his feet</u>, though. He crosses quickly.

____ **3.** It is easy to carry his son. He is <u>used to</u> it.

____ **4.** They were <u>on the go</u> all day, and now they are tired.

____ **5.** They are near their house now. <u>Before long</u>, they will be home.

a. busy

b. soon

c. move slowly

d. accustomed to

e. looks carefully

B. Explain each underlined idiom in your own words.

6. The father is so tired that he is <u>on the verge of</u> falling. _____

7. He will not <u>take it easy</u> until they are safely home, though. _____

8. He wants to be <u>on time</u> for dinner. _____

9. When they arrive home, his son is <u>fast asleep</u>. _____

10. The father puts his son to bed and <u>keeps an eye on</u> the boy while he sleeps.

_____

LITERARY ANALYSIS: Connect Characters and Theme

The theme is the main message of a story. Characters think, feel, say, and do things in a story that give you clues to the theme.

A. Reread "The Gift of the Magi." Find details that give clues to the story's theme. Add those clues to the Character Chart.

Character Chart

Actions	Thoughts and Feelings	Words

B. Discuss the clues with a partner. Explain how they show the theme of "The Gift of the Magi."

C. Now write a short paragraph about the story's theme. Be sure to include the clues that helped you find the theme.

_____

_____

_____

_____

_____

_____

Vocabulary Review

A. Study each picture. Circle the word that completes each sentence.

1.

The scientist brings **(integrity /
wealth)** to her work.

2.

She makes an **(offer / attitude)**
to buy the basket.

3.

The girl rips the paper to
(reflect / reveal) the gift.

4.

His funny **(behavior / success)**
made the students laugh.

B. Choose words to complete the web below. Decide which words name or describe
a person's spirit. (Hint: Think of *a(n)* _____ *spirit* or *a spirit of* _____.) You
will not use every word.

dignity   **honest**   **proud**   **standard**
generosity   **invent**   **sensitive**

Word Web

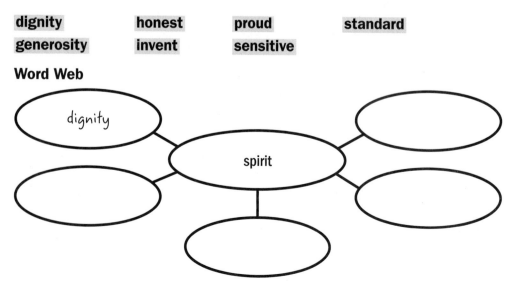

© NGSP & HB

attitude	fair	invent	recognize	sensitive	wealth
behavior	generosity	luck	reflect	spirit	wish
cheat	honest	offer	refuse	standard	
dignity	inspire	precious	reveal	success	
exchange	integrity	proud	sacrifice	tradition	

C. Choose a word that completes each sentence correctly.

| cheat | generosity | precious | refuse | success | wish |
| fair | inspire | recognize | sacrifice | tradition | |

1. Mr. Martin is a _____ teacher. He treats us all the same.

2. "Play by the rules, and do not _____" is good advice.

3. Fire ruined her home, but Aunt Luisa saved her _____ cats.

4. Greg will want to help us. He will not _____ our request.

5. I will _____ my allowance and give the money to charity.

6. The speaker's powerful words always _____ listeners.

7. Tanya's greatest _____ was getting into college.

8. I did not _____ my friend after she got her hair cut.

9. I _____ I could fly like a bird.

10. My family has a _____ of watching movies on Friday nights.

Acknowledgments, continued from page ii

173 ©Chassenet/photocuisine/Corbis. **175** ©Corbis/JupiterImages. **176** ©Jim Bartosik/ The Mazer Corporation. **177** ©Jim Bartosik/ The Mazer Corporation. **179** ©Arena Street Press; ©Arena Street Press; ©Arena Street Press; ©Thinkstock Images/Jupiter Images. **180** ©Arena Street Press; ©Arena Street Press. **181** ©Arena Street Press. **187** © Masterfile. **191** ©Sara Beazley/Debut Art. **193** ©Portrait of Emily Dickinson (**1830-86**) as a Child, from the 'Letters of Emily Dickinson', **1951** (litho), English School, (**20**th century) / Private Collection / The Bridgeman Art Library. **198** ©Corbis/Veer; ©Nonstock/Jupiter Images; Robert Kneschke/ Shutterstock. **200** ©John Feingersh/Getty Images. **205** ©Andrew Holder; ©Andrew Holder. **206** ©Richard I'Anson/Lonely Planet Images. **208** ©Richard I'Anson/Lonely Planet Images. **209** ©Charles Peterson/The Image Bank/ Getty Images. **216** ©Kent Floris. **217** ©Kent Floris. **222** ©Keith Brofsky/UpperCut Images/ Getty Images. **229** ©Blend Images/Alamy. **230** ©James Bentley/Lindgren & Smith; ©James Bentley/Lindgren & Smith. **231** ©James Bentley/ Lindgren & Smith; ©James Bentley/Lindgren & Smith; ©James Bentley/Lindgren & Smith; ©James Bentley/Lindgren & Smith. **233** ©Richard Solomon/Murry Kimber. **234** ©Richard Solomon/ Murry Kimber. **236** ©Richard Solomon/Murry Kimber; ©Ha Lam. **240** ©Stockbyte/Alamy; ©Somos Images LLC/Alamy.